THE BALKANS OVER YEARS

THE BALKANS OVER YEARS

HISTORY AND POLITICS

TAHIR MAHMUTEFENDIC

Copyright © 2018 by Tahir Mahmutefendic.

Library of Congress Control Number: 2018907392
ISBN: Hardcover   978-1-5434-9134-0
              Softcover   978-1-5434-9133-3
              eBook   978-1-5434-9132-6

All rights reserved. No part of this book may be reproduced or transmitted in any form or by any means, electronic or mechanical, including photocopying, recording, or by any information storage and retrieval system, without permission in writing from the copyright owner.

Any people depicted in stock imagery provided by Getty Images are models, and such images are being used for illustrative purposes only.
Certain stock imagery © Getty Images.

Print information available on the last page.

Rev. date: 06/27/2018

To order additional copies of this book, contact:
Xlibris
800-056-3182
www.Xlibrispublishing.co.uk
Orders@Xlibrispublishing.co.uk
781158

CONTENTS

Preface ix

Introduction xi

PART 1 : HISTORY

- Muharem Bazdulj:"The Second Book", Northwestern University Press, Evanston Illinois, USA, 2005 3

- Robert J. Donia:"Sarajevo – A Biography", Hurst & Company, London, 2006 6

- Robin Okey:"TAMING BALKAN NATIONALISM- The Habsburg 'Civilizing Mission' in Bosnia", 1878-1914, Oxford University Press 2007 10

- Paul Mojzes:'Balkan Genocides – Holocaust and Ethnic Cleansing in the Twentieth Century', Rowman & Littlefield Publishers, Plymouth, United Kingdom, 2011, pp299 14

- Alessandro Roselli:'Italy And Albania – Financial Relations In The Fascist Period', I.b. Tauris & Co. Ltd 2006 19

- Rodney Atkinson:"Fascist Europe Rising", Newcastle Upon Tyne; Compuprint Pub, UK 1991 24

- Enver Redzic:"Bosnia and Herzegovina in the Second World War" Frank Cass, London-New York, 2006 41

- Marko Attila Hoare:"The Bosnian Muslims in the Second World War:A History", Hurst & Company, London 2013 47

- Marin Vetma:"Father's pledge – 1944". Latrobe Bookbinding, 2004 53

- Jack Saltman:'KURT WALDHEIM'-A Case to Answer?, Robson Books in association with Channel Four Television Company, London 1988 56

- Robert Bideleux & Ian Jeffries:'The Balkans-A Post-Communist History'. Routledge, London, 2006 61

PART 2 : POLITICS

- Alija Izetbegovi:"Inescapable Questions – Autobiographical Notes" The Islamic Foundation, Leicester, England, 2003, pp 550, ... 67

- The Bosniak – Adil Zulfikarpasic in Dialogue with Milovan Djilas & Nadezda Gace, First published as Bosnjak Adil Zulfikarpasic by the Bosniak Institute, Zurich 1996. First published in the United Kingdom by C. Hurst & Co. (Publishers) Ltd. in 1998, pp 194 71

- Milutin Propadovich:"The Appalling Story of Euro-American Meddling in Yugoslavia", American-Yugoslav Association JADRAN, Milwaukee, Wisconsin, 2003 75

- James Pettifer:"The Kosova Liberation Army – Underground War to Balkan Insurgency, 1948-2001", Hurst & Company 2012, London 81

- Tonny Brems KInudsen and Carsten Bagge Lausten:"Kosovo between War and Peace – Nationalism, Peace-building and International Trusteeship", published by Routledge, OXON, 2006 87

- Michael Waller, Kyril Drezov and Bullent Gokay (editors):"Kosovo – The politics of delusion" Frank Cass Publishers, London 2001 92

- Alaistair Finlan:"The Collapse of Yugoslavia 1991-1999" Osprey Publishing, Oxford, England, 2004 97

- Michael Mandel:"How America Gets Away With MURDER-Illegal Wars, Collateral Damage and Crimes against Humanity", Pluto Press, London 2004 100

- Marko Attila Hoare: "How Bosnia Armed", Saqibooks, London 2004 107

- James Gow: "The Serbian Project and its Adversaries – A Strategy of War Crimes", Hurst & Co. London 2003 113

- Slobodan Markovich, Eric Beckett Weaver and Vukasin Pavlovic (editors):"Challenges to New Democracies in the Balkans", The Associaltion of Fulbright Alumni of Serbia and Montenegro and Cigoja Press in collaboration with the Anglo-Yugoslav Society, Belgrade 2004 120

- Elizabeth Pond 'Endgame in the Balkans – Regime Change, European Style', Brookings Institution Press, 2006 ...125

- Sumatra Bose:'Bosnia after Dayton – Nationalist Partition and International Intervention', Hurst & Company London 2001, pp 295..127

- Neven Andjelic:"Bosnia-Herzegovina, the End of Legacy", Frank Cass Publishers, London 2003 131

- Paul Lowe: "Bosnians", Saqi Books in association with the Bosnian Institute, London 2005 137

- Svetlana Broz: "Dobri ljudi u vremenu zla – Good People in Evil Time", Media Centar "Prelom", Banja Luka, 2003 140

- Vahida Demirovic: "Visage from the Wasteland", Genie Quest Publishing, UK, 1998 143

PREFACE

The book "The Balkans over years – history and politics" is a collection of book reviews written over a period of almost two decades and published in various issues in The South Slav Journal. The books reviewed are multidisciplinary covering economic, social, political, military, historical, linguistic, legal, literary and even psychological and psychoanalitical facets of analysis of complex life in the Balkans. Nevertheless, historical and political aspects prevail. This is the reason that the book is organised in two parts; History and Politics.

Book reviews in the first part are structured in a chronological order of their contents. „The Second Book"covers a period of 3,500 of human history, and as far as the Balkans is concerned the XIX and the XX century.

"Sarajevo – A Biography" touches all periods of the city's history, but focuses on the XX century."

"Taming Balkan Nationalisms" covers a period of the Austro-Hungarian governance in Bosnia and Herzegovina.

Paul Mojzes analyses genocides in the XIX and the XX century Balkans.

Alessandro Rosseli investigates the inter-war political and economic relations beteen Italy and Albania.

"The Fascists Europe Rising" spans over a long period of the European history, but as far as the Yugoslav affairs are concerned focuses on the events in the WWII and links them to the break-up of the country in the early 1990s.

"Bosnia and Herzegovina in the Second World War", "The Bosnian Muslims in the Second World War", "The Father's Pledge",

"Kurt Waldheim-the Case to Answer" cover the period of the WWII, while "The Balkans-the Post-Communist History" focuses on the events which followed the collapse of communism in Eastern Europe, and especially in the Balkans.

The second part is organised along personalities and topics. "Inescapable Questions" and "The Bosniak" are put next to each other to enable a comparison of relevant facts and different opinions related to the same topic.

Propadovich's defense and exoneration of the Serbs for the war and putting the blame on the great powers, especially Germany and the United States is put next to James Pettifer's accusation of Serbs for a teritorial expansion and war crimes.

Two books on Kosovo are put together. "How Bosnia Armed", "The Serbian Project and its Adversaries", "The Collapse of Yugoslavia 1991-1999" and "How America Gets Away with the MURDER" are put next to each other because they link military with political issues.

"The Endgame in the Balkans", and "Challenges to Democracies in the Balkans" are linked because they connect legal and political topics.

"Bosnia after Dayton" and "Bosnia and Herzegovina – the End of a Legacy" are linked because they consider civilisation, philosophy of history and political issues.

"The Bosnians", "Good People in Evil Time", "Visages from the Wasteland" and "The Killing Days" analyse psychological and psychoanalitical side of the political events.

INTRODUCTION

The Balkans is a Turkish word meaning a mountain covered in forest. The region comprises the former Yugoslavia, Romania, Bulgaria, Greece, Albania and the European part of Turkey. The Balkans is one of the three peninsulae in Southern Europe. Unlike the other two, the Iberian and the Apennine, which are religiously and culturally homogenous, the Balkans have always been a crossroads of civilisations and a mosaic of different religions, cultures, nations and ethnicities. This has been the cause of bloody conflicts throughout history. While the other two peninsulae, together with the most of Europe, experienced two types of conflicts, ideological civil wars and inter-state wars, the Balkans in addition witnessed a third type of conflicts, namely inter-ethnic and/or interreligious wars. As is sometimes said, the Balkan nations have the surplus of history. Or to quote Jean Jacques Rousseau: "Lucky are nations who have boring history"

The Balkan nations were not lucky. While Francis Fukoyama declared "The end of history" with the collapse of communism, most of the Balkan nations experienced "History revisited". The bulk of books reviewed is dedicated to the third type of conflict and its precedents.

Richness of history in the Balkans presumes a multitude of events, persons and facts. In such a situation a several questions could be asked. First, do authors take into account all relevant facts or do they deliberately omit some of them which do not suit them? Second, are the facts and criteria chosen objectively, or according to ideological biases? Third, are the facts objectively analysed or is their interpretation subject to ideological biases? Forthly, are the same facts used in analysis of one event or are they chosen according to the conclusion one wants to arrive at? In other words, whether authors aim at objective or subjective research?

Majority of books reviewed represent objective analyses. In minority of books authors are subjective, biased, one-sided and emotionally charged. Disputes revolve around the questions of historical guilts and merits and the number of victims and crimes commited by various factions in conflicts.

The aim of this book is to present a wide range of topics relevant to the Balkans with a view of ubridging the gaps in opinions and arriving at the objective truth.

PART ONE

HISTORY

Muharem Bazdulj: "The Second Book", Northwestern University Press, Evanston Illinois, USA, 2005

The Second Book is a collection of linked stories which cover a period of 3500 years of human history. Unlike many young writers from newly created Balkan states, whose writings are filled with narrow nationalistic views Muharem Bazdulj weaves imagined realities into fiction and fiction into history in search of universal values.

"Tears in Turin" is a story about the last days of Nietzsche's life. The author of *The Antichrist,* the prophet of doom and gloom, who renounces and despises sentimentality and compassion, when seeing a coachman beating a horse with a whip left a hotel, went up to the horse, put his arms around the horse's neck and burst into tears. This marked the first hour of his madness.

"The Poet" is a story about life and work of the famous Bosnian poet Muhamed Dzenetic.

"The Hot Sun's Golden Circle" is a story about the Egyptian pharaoh Amenhotep IV. After marrying his Syrian wife Nefertiti he encountered a new family of gods which his wife brought from a different culture. Confused with a multitude of gods he decided to replace a traditional and ritualistic polytheism with a metaphysical monotheism.

Bazdulj's anti-nationalism is best expressed in the story *A Twilight Encounter.* The author is equally disgusted with the custom of two bitter enemies, Ali-Pasha Rizvanbegovic and Petar Petrovic Njegos, who celebrated their military victories by collecting decapitated heads of their foes. Gardner Wilkinson, while travelling through Herzegovina and Montenegro, took upon himself the noble task of mediating between the two enemies in order to abolish such a barbaric custom. The story finishes with a light touch of irony. The West, appalled by the barbarity of the Balkan tribes, adopted the same custom of decapitating enemies in a technologically more advances form of the guillotine during the French Revolution.

The Story of Two Brothers is a biblical topic translated into a modern environment, this time with William and Henry James as the main characters. William is a renowned physician and a university professor happily married with five children. Henry is single, with strong homosexual inclinations, in eternal search for identity and the meaning of life.

The title of the story *Fiat Iusticia* is the first part of the Latin proverb *Fiat Iusticia pereat mundus – Let there be a justice even if the world must perish*. As the proverb says it seems as if justice is not of this world. The Roman goddess of justice is represented as a blind woman standing over the scales. Scales represent equality and equality is a mathematical concept. In mathematics all numbers are different and at the same time equal. There is only justice in mathematics, but mathematics is abstract and detached from real life. The story has a polyphonic composition in which apparently unrelated events are linked by a Cabbalistic and magical meaning of the number 36 (36 just men in the Jewish religion).

The last story in the book, *A Real Flower for Tomislav Podgorac*, is a biography of a priest, Tomislav Podgajen, an anti-fascist and a Christian socialist, whose life was filled with the two ideals: devotion to God and social justice. He believed that Plato's hermaphrodite soul was divided into two parts, Church and Bolshevism, both of them aiming at the same goal. He dreamt of a success of socialism in Russia, which would be ridden of a militant atheism.

The Second Book is a treasure of knowledge. A whole army of famous philosophers, writers, artists and scientists march through the book. Some names appear in more than one story: Nietzsche, Aristotle, Plato, Michelangelo, da Vinci, Durer, Kundera, Borges, Brodsky, Milosz etc. The influence of Kundera, Borges and Calvino is easily discernible.

The book contains much less known information. Pushkin's great grandfather was an African boy, Obrahim, who was sold at the Istanbul slave market and bought as a present for the Russian Tsar Peter the Great. The word *assassin* in English and French, *assassin* in Italian, for a killer, originates from the Arabic word *hashish* (weed), known in the UK as a *cannabis*. The magical number 36 is a multiple of the number 3, which is holy to Christianity and the number 12, which is holy to Judaism. *No passaran*, a fighting slogan of the Republicans in the Spanish civil war, originates from St. Luke's Gospel.

Highly enjoyable and inspiring, captivating and profoundly intellectual, *The Second Book* is warmly recommended to readers.

Robert J. Donia: "Sarajevo – A Biography", Hurst & Company, London, 2006

Sarajevo attracted attention of the world three times in the XX century. First time in 1914, when Gavrilo Princip assassinated the Austro-Hungarian archduke and the heir of the throne Franz Ferdinand. This triggered off the greatest conflict in the history, known in most of history books as the WWI. Second time in 1984 when it hosted the Winter Olympic Games. The third time between April 1992 and December 1995, when it was under the siege and at the centre of the Bosnian war.

Robert J. Donia spent three years in Sarajevo during the 1970's. He returned to the city in 1994, where ever since he spent several weeks every year. During his stay in Sarajevo he conducted thorough research of the city's history. The book *Sarajevo-A biography* emerged as a result of his detailed and exhaustive work.

According to the author the book is a political history titled as a biography. It is a story of the city told in a chronological order, from its foundation by Ishakbeg Isakovic in 1460 to the present. The book is divided into ten chapters, each of them representing a distinguished period in the city's history. Introduction comprises the foundation of the city and the Ottoman rule. A second chapter deals with the Sarajevo uprising and the advent of the Habsburg rule. A third chapter 'The Making of *Fin de Siecle* Sarajevo' explores a development of the city as a part of the Austro-Hungarian empire from the occupation in 1878 until the end of the XIX century. A chapter entitled 'The New Nationalism, Assassination, and War' deals with the period from the beginning of the XX century until the end of the WWI. A fifth chapter 'Royal Yugoslavia's Forgotten City investigates a period between the two world wars. A chapter 'Occupation and Urban Resistance in the Second World War' is a story about the life in the city under the Nazi and Ustasha occupation. Chapters cover 'Sarajevo under Socialism' and 'From Socialist Decline to Sarajevo's National Division' cover the city's history from the end of the WWII to the beginning of the Bosnian war in 1992. Chapters 'Death and Life in Sarajevo under Siege' and 'Sarajevo in the Long Shadow of War' describe the siege of Sarajevo and the aftermath of the war.

The author explains that every ruler of the Sarajevo had a strategy related to the city's role. The Ottomans envisioned Sarajevo as a city in the service of Islam and as a crossroad of their military campaigns. Although Muslims were privileged the authorities espoused tolerance and left enough space for other religious communities; Orthodox, Catholic and Jewish. Under the Habsburg rule Sarajevo expanded its territory and developed into a modern European city, blending its newly acquired Western values with the Oriental heritage. Through the joint finance minister Benjamin Kalay, who governed Bosnia and Herzegovina for the most of the period of the empire's rule, the Habsburgs tried to promote multi-confessional Bosnian nationality in order to curb Serb and Croat nationalism. As a part of the Kingdom of Serbs, Croats and Slovenes and later the Kingdom of Yugoslavia Sarajevo experienced decline. This was the result of the world depression and over-centralised political system. The sheer title of the state favoured Belgrade, Zagreb and Ljubljana, who received three times more many per inhabitant for their city's budget than Sarajevo. Apart from using the city's industrial facilities and infrastructure Nazi and Ustasha wanted to destroy the Jewish and to a lesser degree the Serb community. Although Sarajevo did not experience physical destruction it suffered huge human losses. More than 10,000 Sarajevans (11% of the prewar population) perished in the WWII, 65% of them Jews. Communist authorities tried to exploit their victory in the WWII and the policy of 'Brotherhood and unity' to attract Sarajevans to socialist ideology. They succeded in doing so in the first two decades of their rule when Sarajevo experienced an unprecedented prosperity. A deterioration of economic situation in Yugoslavia, i.e.

huge external debt, high unemployment and hyperinflation shaken the belief in the communist ideology, replacing it by the rising tide of nationalism. The Bosnian Serb nationalists wanted to divide the city into a Muslim and Serb part with the intention to wipe out any trace of a common life. With that view they put the pressure and sometimes threatened Sarajevo Serbs to live the city. After the war ruling Bosniak and Croat nationalist parties, although paying a lip service to a common life, undermine it with their policies. The exception is a period between 2000 and 2002, when the social democrats won the elections in the city

Robert Donia describes the situation in Sarajevo after the war with these words:" The contrast with recovery after the Second World War could not have been greater. The triumphant Partisans had given Sarajevans a clear if idealized vision of a new society and a transformed city to be constructed in the aftermath of the war and liberation. In 1996, however, there was no sense of victory, no inspiring vision to compel popular engagement in remaking the city. War was over, but the struggle was not resolved. With international blessing, the Dayton Agreement institutionalised many of the national divisions that had dominated society since 1990. Most Sarajevans were immensely relieved that the war had ended, but a widespread sense of uncertainty about the future fed pervasive lassitude and despair, despite the gradual return of intense activity to the central city".

The war changed an ethno-national structure of the city's population. Some Croats and more than 100,000 Serbs left the city. They were replaced by 90,000 Bosniaks from East Bosnia, expelled by the Serb nationalists. The Dayton agreement and the international community encouraged a return of refugees. Sarajevo was in the lead of such an effort with ¼ of all refugees returning after the war. Most of them were Serbs and Croats. As a result the percentage of Bosniaks in Sarajevo canton fell from 87% in 1996 to 75% in 2005. Robert Donia claims that although there are still strong elements of a common life in the city its future is uncertain.

The book is written as a thesis. The central thesis is that the city and its people became more diverse, tolerant and consequently more prosperous when they have been governed by a single inclusive vision. The Ottomans, the Habsburgs and the communists at the peak of their power succeeded to deliver prosperity to the city before internal crisis and external pressure brought their reign to an end. In that respect, according to the author, the city has benefited from immigration. The immigration of peasants in the XV and XVI century, the arrival of Sephardic Jews in the XVI century, the immigration of administrators and various professionals during the Habsburg rule and the influx of newcomers after the WWI and WWII brought the city fresh blood, new skills and contributed to its overall prosperity. Consequently, the city became less prosperous, less diverse and tolerant in the periods of sectarian rule and non-inclusive policies.

Robert Donia used a wide variety of resources; archive sources, primary documents and document collections, books and articles. The most resources are in Bosnian/Serbo-Croat, but some of them are also in German and French. The book is a treasure of knowledge about Sarajevo and its history. Although primarily written as a political history, the book does not neglect economic, legal and artistic, especially architectural aspect of the city's past and present. The book is warmly recommended to readers.

Robin Okey:"TAMING BALKAN NATIONALISM-The Habsburg 'Civilizing Mission' in Bosnia", 1878-1914, Oxford University Press 2007

As the title indicates the book "TAMING BALKAN NATIONALISM-The Habsburg' Civilizing Mission' in Bosnia, 1878-1914" is about occupation and annexation of Bosnia and Herzegovina by the Austro-Hungarian Empire. In a memorandum to the European great powers of 21. April 1878 the Austro-Hungarian foreign minister Gyula Andrassy made a case for the Habsburg occupation of Bosnia and Herzegovina. He pointed out that Bosnia and Herzegovina was not equipped for autonomous development. A great power was therefore needed to bring prosperity, the rule of law and above everything to carry out a cultural mission in the country which was as backward as some of European external colonies after more than four centuries of the Ottoman rule. Behind these altruistic outpours a high policy is easily revealed. By occupying Bosnia and Herzegovina and in the view of the Russian victory over the Ottoman Empire in 1877 Austro-Hungary wanted to curb Slav nationalism and prevent the formation of a large South Slav state.

The best person to carry out the Empire's mission was Benjamin von Kallay. A descendant of Hungarian nobility, brought up by a Magyarised Serb mother, Kallay was an expert in Serb affairs. He was the Empire's Consul General in Belgrade from 1868 to 1874. During this period Kallay tried to forge the alliance between Serbs and Hungarians, revolved around the plan of the establishment of 'The

Danubian Confederation'. He also wrote a book 'The *History of Serbs in Bosnia and Herzegovina* ', which he later renounced.

Kallay's administration of Bosnia and Herzegovina marks the longest period of the Austro-Hungarian occupation of Bosnia and Herzegovina from its beginning in 1878 to his death in 1903. The main characteristic of his strategy was the promotion of the Bosnian nationhood. By doing this Kallay wanted to cushion Serb and Croat nationalism and facilitate a smooth integration of the province in the Empire. History textbooks paid a special attention to history of the medieval Bosnian kingdom with the view of raising the Bosnian national conscience. Kallay treated the Slav population of Bosnia and Herzegovina as Bosnians of three faiths. Religious and cultural autonomy was promoted to emphasize religious, rather than national sentiments among Serbs and Croats. Kallay regarded Bosnian begs as the pillar of such a strategy considering them the descendants of medieval Bosnian Bogumil aristocracy. However, he did not abandon hopes that Muslims, detached from an Islamic superpower, will eventually return to Christianity.

Kallay was replaced by Istvan Burian, who governed Bosnia and Herzegovina from 1903 to 1912. During this period cultural institutions among all the three communities mushroomed. Burian was also seeking rapprochement to Serbs. This was not the result of his Serbophilia, but a pragmatic approach aimed at diverting Bosnian and Herzegovinian Serbs from Serbia. At the same time Burian intensified government control of cultural and educational institutions, which made him unpopular, especially among Serbs.

Burian was replaced by Oskar von Potiorek in 1912. In his policy he combined a long-term strategic goal of crushing Serbia with an attempt to attract as many Serbs as possible in political life, especially in the Diet.

In a general assessment of the Austro-Hungarian policy in Bosnia and Herzegovina Professor Okey recognised that the Empire had faced an awesome task in its mission. He stated that its policy of economic and industrial development was relatively successful, although the unresolved agrarian question (it was also unresolved in many other parts of the Empire, e.g. Hungary) left a vast majority of peasants in abject poverty with their standard of living almost stagnant.

Professor Okey gives more credit to the Empire's educational policy. State-backed common schools for all the three communities established a long lasting basis for the integration of the Bosnian communities. The biggest success derived from such an educational policy was the emergence of a small educated Muslim elite imbibing the Western system of values to its community. In historical perspective this laid grounds to the evolution of the modern Bosniak nation.

Professor Okey's assessment of the Austro-Hungarian national policy is less favourable. He states that Kallay overestimated his skills and that promotion of Bosnian nation and denial of Serbdom and Croatdom in Bosnia was like a red rag to a bull.

In his overall assessment of the Austro-Hungarian record in Bosnia and Herzegovina Professor Okey makes comparison with the period of a communist rule. Similar in duration the both periods witnessed relative economic prosperity and progress in education. However, the both system of governing failed to solve the national question.

Austro-Hungarian administration in Bosnia and Herzegovina faced two irresoluble problems. Its civilizing mission ran out of steam when Serb and Croat nationalists embraced the European system of values. They claimed that their quest for modernity and prosperity was more valid since it excluded an alien rule. Second, promotion of civic versus ethnic nationalism was contested by Serb and Croat nationalist. Serb and Croat intelligensia and burgeoning burgeois class, as bearers of national conscience, claimed that their nationalism was civic and not ethnic, by treating all the three communities as Serbs and Croats of three faiths respectively. The Empires administrators realized that they were not dealing with backward Orientals of three faiths but with a modern nationalism of the Central European type. Eventually, the Austro-Hungarian Empire as a supra-national entity lost its appeal and was replaced after the WWI by nation states which could cater better for collective identities of their constituent peoples.

The book contains much of the archival work which Professor Okey had undertaken for his doctoral thesis, defended at Oxford University in 1972. Ever since he has published extensively on the topic. The book represents a crown work of his research. It contains almost 500 sources. They consist of unpublished and published sources such as books, articles, newspapers, periodicals and secondary sources. Professor Okey has used sources in six languages:English, Bosnian/Serbo-Croat, German, French, Hungarian and Italian. Bibliography is impressive and represents an invaluable database for professional historians who would be interested to carry out a research on the similar topics. The book will also appeal to a non-professional reader interested in the modern history of the South-East Europe.

Paul Mojzes: 'Balkan Genocides – Holocaust and Ethnic Cleansing in the Twentieth Century', Rowman & Littlefield Publishers, Plymouth, United Kingdom, 2011, pp299

The book represents a comprehensive study off all genocides committed in the Balkans in the twentieth century. The opening chapter entitled 'Definition of Genocide and Ethnic Cleansing' deals with various definitions and explanations of genocide, ethnic cleansing, persecution, extermination, massacre and mass murder. Although the UN Convention on the Prevention and Punishment of the Crime of Genocide of 1948 remains the official definition of genocide it has been criticized as being too narrow, since it does not include politicide, and too broad at the same time, because it does not specify how small or large targeted group should be to qualify as a victim of genocide. Professor Mojzes considers the more recent definition of genocide by ICTY more adequate. According to this definition there must be intent to destroy a sizable group of targeted population in order to consider the action genocide. Also, when destruction is intended only against a specified or localised part of a group it is still to be classified as genocide. Following this definition a massacre of 7,000-8,000 Muslim men captured in Srebrenica by the Serb army constitutes genocide.

Genocides are analysed in detailed and exhaustive study in a chronological order. The analysis starts with genocides committed in the Balkan wars and during the WWI, including the genocide of Armenians in 1915 and the genocides committed in the aftermath of the WWI in the Greek-Turkish wars. This is followed by genocides committed during the WWII by the occupying forces and their domestic collaborators. Then retaliatory ethnic cleansing and genocides against Germans, Hungarians and Italians in the aftermath of the WWI by victorious partisans is analysed. One chapter is devoted to Bleiburg and the fate of Ustashas and other military collaborators of the Axis forces. Professor Mojzes concludes that this was not the case of genocide, but politicide.

The largest part of the book deals with the most recent ethnic cleansing and genocides during the wars for the Yugoslav succession in Croatia, Bosnia and Herzegovina and Kosovo. In this section professor Mojzes discusses contentious analytical issues related to causes of these wars. He puts the potential causes of the wars in a binary opposition:1. Complex versus simple reasons, 2. Ancient hatreds versus contemporary political ambitions of leaders, 3. Wars of aggression versus civil wars, 4. Intra-Yugoslav crisis versus foreign meddling, 5. National versus ethnic wars and 6. Religious versus secular wars. Professor Mojzes correctly concludes that the wars had elements of both, aggression and civil war. As regards of secular or religious character of the wars he comes up with an interesting statement that these were religious wars fought by irreligious people. A similar statement was declared by a Serbian Orthodox priest from Birmingham who said that these were religious wars waged by atheists. These conclusions are in accordance with the attitudes of most researches who tried to find out an explanation of the role of religion amongst predominantly irreligious population. They found a solution in Rousseau's concept of civil religion, where religious statements are used one-off for the sake of political expedience. In this respect there is a similarity with Zionists. Although the founders of the Zionist movement were resolutely non-religious they sometimes repeated that God gave the Jews the Promised Land.

Professor Mojzes espouses a balanced, nuanced and subtle approach. This is particularly pronounced in his analysis of intra-ethnic conflicts and the attitude of the Bulgarian government to the Jews during the WWII. A narrative is a combination of scholarly and a story-telling style. This makes the book livelier and more interesting to read.

The book contains a couple of minor inaccuracies. On page 166 a sentence reads:" *The Croats and Muslims of Mostar were, roughly speaking, equally numerous and the Serbs* were *a large minority.*" According to the census of population in 1991 Muslims made up 44 per cent and Croats 25 per cent of Mostar's population.

On page 168 a sentence reads:" *The largest number of Croats lived in Herzegovina.*" It should be the largest percentage. In absolute numbers there were 175,000 Croats in Herzegovina and around 600,000 in Bosnia before the war.

In a several places professor Mojzes mentions claims and statements of some authors without mentioning their names and sources.

The book contains a several contentious issues and statements. On page 46 professor Mojzes mentions that "*Using the name Jasenovac as a symbol, many Serbs overreached by rejecting the very idea of an independent Croatian state and regarded all who favoured the idea-including the Roman Catholic Church and the Vatican, which provided support to that state-as being guilty of genocide.*" Paradoxically, Vatican never recognised the Independent State of Croatia and Niko Barosevic, a representative of the Yugoslav government in exile had his office in Vatican throughout the war.

On pages 49 and 127 professor Mojzes states that Franjo Tudjman undermined the number of victims in Jasenovac and tried to even them out with the number of victims in Bleiburg. He corroborates his statement by using a revised version of Tudjman's book:"Horrors of War:Historical Reality and Philosophy", translated from Croatian by Katarina Mijatovic and published in New York in 1996 by M. Evans. I read the original version in Croatian entitled:"Bespuca povijesne zbilje", which could be literally translated as 'Wastelands of Historical Reality'. Tudjman claims that 60,000 of citizens of Croatia perished in Jasenovac. This is corroborated with other researches, including Ivo Goldstein. If the whole of the Independent state of Croatia is taken into account, which comprised Bosnia and Herzegovina and Western Srem/Srijem as well then he thinks that the number of victims should be multiplied by 3-4. Therefore, Tudjman estimates the number of killed in Jasenovac between 180,000 and 240,000, which is in accordance with the estimates of most of serious historians including

Bogoljub Kocovic, who is mentioned on page 49. The only exception is Vladimir Zerjavic, who estimates the number of victims in Jasenovac between 77,000 and 83,000.

On page 85 it is mentioned that 50,000 died in Belgrade when Germany bombarded it on 6th April 1941. Belgrade had a population of 250,000, so it was impossible even for the Luftwafe to kill 20 per cent of all inhabitants in one day. The highest figure I came across was by Tudjman, 17,000, which included the number of victims of bombardment and in collateral damage.

On page 123 it was mentioned that Italy was on the "wrong" side of World War I and that this was the reason why it lost most of Dalmatia. Italy actually was on the winning side since it swapped sides and joined the Antante in 1915. It was on the "wrong" side for a year or so but it is unclear whether it was relevant in post war allocation of territories.

Contentious is also the reading of "Islamic Declaration". Izetbegovic never mentioned that his aim was the establishment of an Islamic state in Bosnia. He repeated a several times that there aim was islamisation of Muslims, who were highly secular after the WWII and are still very secular compared to the Muslims in most of the world.

All these contentious issues and statements represent strength more than a weakness of the book. They inspire polemics, debates and future research on the topics. The most contentious statement could be found on page 1:*"If there were "bragging rights" for being a genocidal and ethnic cleansing area, the Balkans could claim championship status".*

If destruction of part of a group on political and ideological grounds is included the question is whether Guernica, the massacre of 1800 civilians in the Republican town of Badajoz in only 12 hours by the Maroccan regiments and a slaughter of a several thousand captured nationalistic soldiers in Republican held prisons in Madrid constitute genocide. If so then seven million dead claimed by the Russian civil war and half a million claimed by the Spanish Civil War would deprive the Balkan peoples of the "honour" of being the champions in genocide. The statement is also very inspiring in connection with the claim, mentioned in the book, that most of wars are religious and that religious people consider themselves morally superior compared to irreligious individuals. Atheists usually say:"If religion is that good why did it produce so much evil?" Religious leaders and scholars strike back claiming that atheists committed more crimes than religious people. In order to further their cause they classify Hitler as an atheist. It would be very interesting to conduct a thorough research which would give an answer to a crucial question; who committed more crimes throughout history:Religious fanatics or atheists, blind followers of intransigent and intolerant secular ideologies?

Alessandro Roselli:'Italy And Albania – Financial Relations In The Fascist Period', I.b. Tauris & Co. Ltd 2006

The motto of the book "…….. *timeo Danaos et dona ferentes*" (I am afraid of the Greeks even when they bring gifts), borrowed from Virgil's Aeneid, succinctly describes the relationship between Italy and Albania in the interwar period. Despite of a heavy Italian involvement in Albanian political, economic and financial affairs Albania did not benefit at all in terms of economic and social progress. While at the beginning of the XX century Italian GDP per capita was less than four times higher than GDP per capita in Albania it was almost six times higher at the end of the 1930's. Although the data on macroeconomic performance are scarce they show that from 1926 to 1938 the Albanian economy grew by 12%, at an average annual rate of less than 1%. At the same time population increased by 26%. This means that GDP per capita and the standard of living fell in real terms. While this phenomenon could be partly explained by the negative effects of the Great Depression, it shows more about real intentions of the Italian government regarding its Albanian policy. The main reason behind economic stagnation Rosseli finds in a lack of industrialisation. Mussolini wanted deliberately to preserve predominantly rural structure of the Albanian economy and society fearing that industrial development will lead to a rise in the urban working class and the opposition to the fascist regime. In addition Italy wanted the Albanian economy to be complementary to the Italian economy. Albania was supposed to produce primary products and Italy industrial manufacturing goods.

Fascist propaganda praised the Italian involvement in Albania, pointing out that the Albanian national currency franc was the strongest and the most stable in Europe, that the government budget was balanced and that overall balance of payments was in surplus despite the fact that both trade account and current account of the balance of payments were heavily in deficit. A large flow of capital from Italy to Albania was aimed at stabilisation not development. As a result the structure of the Albanian economy and society remained rural, with a high rate of illiteracy and a low proportion of educated persons. Real income, GDP and the standard of living were low and Albania remained by far the poorest country in Europe. At the same time Italy did not benefit economically from its heavy involvement in Albanian affairs. Political and military aims took the precedence over economic and financial considerations. In the long run the fascist government in Rome wanted to make Albania an Italian colony, *La Quinta Sponda d'Italia* – The fifth shore of Italy or part of *L'Iitalia d'Oltramare*– overseas Italy.

The book covers a period from 1900 to the capitulation of Italy in 1943. Political history of Albania is intertwined with financial and economic developments. At the beginning of the XX century Albania was still part of the Ottoman Empire. It was fragmented along clan and social lines. Its economy was backward and a middle class, usually the bearer of national consciences and national identity, weak and undeveloped. These drawbacks were offset by external developments; disintegration of the Ottoman Empire and increasing interest of two superpowers, Austro-Hungarian Empire and Italy in Albanian affairs. The both countries wanted an independent Albanian state, Austro-Hungarian Empire because it wanted to contain Slavic nationalism and Italy because it wanted to increase its cultural, political and economic influence in the region. Albanian independence came into fruition after the first Balkan war in 1912 and it was internationally confirmed at the London conference in 1913. Before the WWI Austro-Hungarian Empire was Albania's main trading partner, but after its dissolution Italy took over.

After the WWI it was realised that the young state could hardly be viable without strong external support. The League of Nations endorsed Italy to be the major supporter of Albania's independence. In the first half of the 1920's Italy showed a great involvement in Albanian affairs. Italian engagement came from the government and did not attract private capital, except a few speculators. This involvement culminated in 1925 with the establishment of the National Bank of Albania and SVEA (Societa per svilupo economico dell'Albania – Society for economic development of Albania), whose aim was to finance public works, but who ended up financing the government budget deficit and a deficit on the current account of the balance of payments. Internal developments witnessed the government of Mgsr. Fan Noli, the red priest whose government was one of the few at the time to recognise the Soviet Union in 1924, being replaced by more conservative Ahmed Zog in 1925. The latter was the Prime Minister in 1925, the president of the Republic in 1926 and proclaimed himself the king in 1928.

Albanian Marxist historiography is full of praise for Fan Noli, who wanted an independent Albania and accused Ahmed Zog for selling the country to Italy. This assessment is backed by the developments related to the establishment of the National Bank of Albania. With the establishment of the bank the pure gold standard was replaced by the gold exchange standard. According to the official historiography the main aim of the change in the monetary system was to collect gold stock held by Albanian citizens, exchange it for banknotes and siphon off the gold to Italy. At the same time the official historiography claimed that the main source of funds was not Italian capital, but remittances from Albanian emigrants living abroad. In fact Ahmed Zog was sitting on the fence, changing allegiances between Yugoslavia, Italy and Great Britain. According to more balanced assessment Ahmed Zog's personal expenditure and development plans did not match available resources. This is why he was desperate to obtain money from whichever source he could.

Increased inflow of Italian capital enabled Albania to change the geographical structure of its foreign trade. While Italy remained the main destination for its exports Albania diversified its imports, buying much more goods from third countries. As a result a huge trade deficit with Italy was turned into a surplus.

The fascist government was not happy with such development. Faced by difficulties in its own economy, caused by the Great Depression and unsatisfied with the results of its involvement in Albania, Italy significantly reduced exports of capital to Albania. This prompted Ahmed Zog to rely on other countries, causing a tension in relationship with Rome. Although a temporary reconciliation was achieved in 1936, Italy eventually decided to occupy and annex Albania in April 1939. Ahmed Zog fled the country and emigrated to Greece.

After the annexation Italy aimed to establish economic, customs and monetary union between the two countries and to reverse negative trends in trade balance with Albania. It undertook several projects in extraction of mineral resources, building infrastructure, land reclamation and property development. The projects were motivated by strategic goals and were not profitable. War efforts diverted attention from Albania. The fascist government plan to develop a sound economic strategy in Albania after the war.

The largest part of the book is devoted to the analysis of the financial developments in Albania in the interwar period. The whole chapters are allocated to the creation of the National Bank of Albania, trade balance, the balance of payments, prices, exchange rates, monetary systems and monetary policy. Non-expert readers might not be familiar with professional terms and concepts such as balance sheet, assets, liabilities, bimetallism, gold bullion and gold-exchange standard, real and nominal exchange rate, restrictive and monetary policy. However, economic and political analysis which accompanies the analysis of financial developments as well as the conclusion are written in the language accessible to a non-expert reader.

Alessandro Roselli is the Chief Representative in the United Kingdom of the central Bank of Italy where he has spent the whole of his carrier. He is therefore an extremely competent expert in the topic he chose for his book. Roselli has conducted a detailed, meticulous and highly sophisticated analysis of the financial, political and economic relations between Italy and Albania in the interwar period. The book

'Italy and Albania – Financial Relations in the Fascist Period' will attract attention of the expert readers. It might also appeal to non-expert readers interested in the modern European history. The book is warmly recommended to readers.

Rodney Atkinson:"Fascist Europe Rising", Newcastle Upon Tyne; Compuprint Pub, UK 1991

The title of the book „Fascist Europe Rising"immediately attracts the attention of the readers. Before opening the book readers probably expect the pages of the book to be filled with a detailed analysis of far right-wing movements in Western Europe such as Neo-Nazi organisations in Germany, the BNP in the UK, the National Front in France and similar extreme nationalist and fascist political parties in Eastern Europe. In fact, the book deals with the major European economic and political project, the European Union. The author, Rodney Atkinson, describes the whole project of the European Union creation as a fascist. A former member of Conservative Party, Referendum Party candidate in the 1997 election and Independent Party candidate in 1999 local election, he is a staunch opponent not only of the Euro, but of the European Union altogether. His arguments could be summarised as follows:

1. The peoples of Western Europe have been enticed to join the European Economic Community by promising a free trade in goods and services between the member countries. The idea of liberalisation of trade which brought lower prices, increased consumer surplus, wider choice and better quality of goods and services looked to good to be resisted and the electorate in many Western European countries cast a „Yes"vote in referendum whether to join the economic association. Voters

were given a firm guarantees that EEC membership would not infringe on national independence and that full national sovereignty would be retained. According to the author this was a clever concocted trick whose aim was to take away national sovereignty of the free nations of Europe and transfer it to the giant European superstate. Slowly and gradually unelected and unaccountable politicians and bureaucrats, backed by big multinational corporations, introduced laws, rules and regulations which curbed the power of national parliaments and handed the decision making process to the institutions of the future federal European state. The author lists several allegedly devious techniques, which have been used to destroy the nation states which he equates with freedom and democracy. The first of these techniques has been secrecy and deceit, since the true aims of the *Eurofederalists* could never be revealed. The second technique has been to create the impression of inevitability with concommitant technique of the „deadline method". The third technique has arisen conveniently out of the fact that 15 member states could never agree a clear and specific wording of any treaty. As a result the European Court of Justice is entitled to interpret the treaties and to make laws in the interests of the new central state against the sovereign interests of the constituent nations. The fourt technique is „ the pragmatic interest group"technique which overrides the rights of European nation states for the sake of efficiency in solving differences between member countries. The fifth technique is never to discuss the next anti-democratic step in the destruction of national democracies until that stage had already effectively been achieved. The sixth, the most insidious of all, is the technique of inserting into every aspect of a nation's life the insignia of the imperial power (the stars of the European Union flag). The author gives numerous examples in which these techniques were applied with the effect of surrending the power of the national authorities to the institutions of the European Union.

2. The European Union brings together, under the umbrella of the one super state, nations with subtle, but unbridgeable

cultural, psychological and linguistic differences. The Euro imposes common monetary, fiscal, social and other economic policies on incompatible national economies with different economic structures and huge differences in the level of development. These countries have different patterns of business cycle and require different policies to achieve major macroeconomic objectives such as high growth, low unemployment, low inflation and external balances. For example, if a country has high unemployment it needs to lower interest rates and taxes and increase public spending in order to boost aggregate demand. On the other hand if a country has high inflation it needs to do exactly the opposite; to increase interest rates and taxes and to reduce public expenditure. If phases of the business cycle are not synchronised between the member countries and if economic policy measures are decided in one centre it can happen that a country with a high unemployment might be forced to accept an increase in interest rates and taxes and decrease in public expenditure, the meaures which would lead to even higher unemployment. The economic policy measures will inevitably reflect interests of the largest, most developed and most powerful members of the European Union.

The first step towards a single currency is a fixed exchange rate between national currencies. Fixed exchange rates do not reflect the reality of the exchange markets. A distorted picture is then transferred to capital, financial and babour markets leading to an inefficient allocation of resources. A short membership of ERM brought the UK into a dire position. Billions of pounds were wasted to prop up the pound against the DM and the UK eonomy plunged into a deep recession.

A comparative analysis of Western European economies give Atkinson additional ammunition in slating the whole project of the EU and especially the Euro. He classifies the Western European countries into three groups; countries which accepted the Euro, the EU members which retained their their national currencies and countries which are not the EU members. Comparing the UK with the Euro zone he states that the former had much better economic performance; higher growth, lower unemployment, stronger currency and a vigorous rise in inward investment. The best performances had emanated from Switzerland and Norway, the countries which are not EU members. They are the richest countries in the world and their citizens enjoy the best quality of life.

3. Atkinson espouses a modified Spenglerian world view according to which history repeats itself in cycles. The concept of United Europe is not new and according to Atkinson is German and Catholic in its nature. The first attempt to create a united Europe occurred in the 8th and 9th centuries under the Frankish emperor Charlemagne. The attempt was accompanied by massive killings and forcible conversion of pagans, who lived east of Rhineland, to Christianity. In 800 AD Charlemagne was crowned in Rome „The Roman emperor of the German nation". The second attempt was made by Hitler and the Nazis before and during the second world war. The attempt resulted in tens of millions of dead, concentration camps, genocide and material destruction in the greatest part of the European continent. The third attempt to create a German dominated Europe is the European Union. The attempt intensified after the re-unification of Germany. It was followed by the break-up of Czechoslovakia and the break-up of Yugoslavia through the bloody war.

Atkinson gives many examples which prove a striking similarity in the political rhetoric of Adolf Hitler and Helmut Kohl. A French adage „*plus ca change plus c'est la meme chose*"is the best description of a modified German „*Drang nach Osten*"policy. Atkinson blames the CAP (Common Agricultural Policy), which serves ideally German interests in that respect. Relatively poor Eastern and Central European countries are denied access to the European Union market for agricultural products, which prevents them from exploiting their comparative advantage. Only the EU membership can enable Eastern and Central European countries a fair treatment in the EU market. But the EU membership means that these countries must surrender their hardly won national sovereignty to German dominated structure of the EU. This will be accompanied by numerous legal binding agreements which enable German nationals, former citizens of Eastern and Central European countries, expelled after the Second World War, to reclaim their rights, this time as „European citizens". „*Drang nach Osten*"is preceded by numerous cultural events, societes of friendship etc, strikingly reminiscent of similar occurrencies in the 1930's.

Atkinson stresses that according to a new law all „The European citizens"can be extradited without a trial to Germany. The same does not apply to Germans. A similar law was applied in Nazi occupied Europe.

The book raises many questions which need to be answered.

1. Atkinson attacks the European Union as undemocratic and fascist and praises nation states, equating them with freedom, democracy and the rule of law. In the beginning of the book he quotes the Oxford Dictionary which defines a nation as a „distinct people organised as a separate state". This definition is narrow, Euro-centric and does not have universal meaning, since it can be applied only to a minority of peoples and states. There are more than 1000 peoples in the world and less than 200 states. This means that a vast majority of peoples (more than 80%) do not live in monolithic nation states. This people could be divided into three groups:

   a) The first and the smallest is the group of peoples who live in multi-ethnic or multi-national states and who by constitution particpate in sovereignty of their state. After the break-up of the Soviet Union, Czechoslovakia and Yugoslavia there are only three states in Europe in which their constituent peoples have, at least in theory, equal participation in sovereignty of their state; Switzerland, Belgium and Bosnia and Herzegovina.

   b) The second and much larger group are stateless peoples and those who live outside their mother countries and who have a recognised status as a national minority, but do not participate in the sovereignty of their state. The best example in this group are Basques and all peoples who live outside their mother countries.

c) The third group are stateless peoples who not only do not participate in sovereignty of their state but are not even recognised as a national minority and are not mentioned in a constitution of the stae in which they live. The best examples of this group are Kurds in Turkey and Gypsies throughout Europe.

d) It is obvious that out of more than 80% of peoples who do not live in monolithic nation states only a few of them participate in sovereignty of their states. It is not clear how Atkinson considers this state of affairs preferable. Peoples who belong to other two groups would certainly like to see their states integrated into a large European state. This would give them a chance to enjoy equal rights as all other citizens of Europe. In other words United Europe resolves the problem of national minorities.

2. Atkinson claims that united Europe poses a threat to the 800 years old British democratic constitution. Magna Carta in 1215 was a progressive document since it restricted the power of the king and strenghtened the power of the parliament. However, parliament at that time consisted mainly of the nobility and the vast majority of the population did not have any influence on its functioning. But the more important thing is that it has never been British, but an English constitution. The Welsh and Irish were brought under Magna Carta by sword, not by a democratic decision of their people. The situation is different with the Scots since the unification with England was a voluntary when the Scottish King James VI became the English King James I in 1603. But when in 1707 the Scottish parliament was abolished and when in 1714 the Hanover dynasty took over the British throne Scotts, rebelled and bloody conflict followed. Today more than 50% of Scots would like to join the European super-state not as part of the UK but as an independent state. In such a situation

the restoration of the Scottish parliament and internal self-determination without seccession looks the most sensible solution. However, Atkinson considers this a „creation of petty nationalistic and religious state"(it is not clear on what basisi religious).

Similar undemocratic methods were used in the creation of many other nation states in Europe. Germany was unified by the iron fist of Bismarck, who excluded Austria fearing that the latter might upstage Prussia and become the strongest state in the German Empire. In the XIX century peasants and fishermen in Sicily and Sardinia did not have any feeling of unity with wealthy industrialists and merchants in Piedmont and Lombardy. In other words there was no such a thing as Italian national conscience. This was imposed by a clique of politicians and intellectuals. Following Atkinson's logic and language Germany and Italy could be dubbed „fascist creations of Otto von Bismarck and Camilo Cavur".

3. On page 67 Atkinson writes that „despite our decline since joining the EEC in 1972. during the 1990's (because the United Kingdom opted out of Europe's social chapter, (up to 1997 and the economic straitjackets of the Exchange Rate Mechanism and the Euro) Britons enjoyed unprecedented period of economic growth. While other EU countries suffered years of mass unemployment, huge debts and (up to 1998) little growth, Britain flourished. British industrial workers became the richest in the EU and while the other countries had 6 years of stagnation and unemployment the British enjoyed economic growth and even lower unemployment".

Atkinson did not explain to the readers that the UK opted out of three of 12 clauses of the Social Chapter. The most important clause that the UK opted out of is the clause which restricts the working week to 48 hours. The Conservative government of John Major argued that this would be against labour market flexibility. Labour market flexibility means among other things that employers can force employees to work as many hours as they want. With trade unions seriously weakened during the reign of, by Atkinson, the much praised

Prime Minister Margaret Thatcher this has opened the door to the restoration of slavery, which was officially abolished in 1865 when the civil war in the USA ended. Increased workload, increased pressure on employees, bullying and harrassment and unsanctioned violation of human rights in a work place are modern versions of flogging. „German fascists"and their collaborators on the European continent have so far protected their employees from slavery.

Atkinson would argue that labour market flexibility protected jobs of low-skilled workers and that because of that the UK had lower unemployment than continental European countries. This is true. However, lower unemployment in the UK has its high price:

a) Many low-paid workers in the UK are part-time workers who are employed 1-3 days a week. With their income they can barely cover 20% of their expenses. The rest is covered by the state. If these workers had been treated as essentially unemployed, which they are, the comparative position of the UK would not have been that favourable.

b) Labour market flexibility often forces people to accept any job. There is a popular phrase „work is nobility"which does not differ much from the similar cynical euphemistic inscriptions at the entrance of the Nazi concentration camps"*Arbeit Macht Frei*". As a result 30% employees in the UK are overqualified. It is not rare that cleaners and receptionist are much better educated than their managers. It is not necessary to explain what a waste of human resources such a situation creates.

c) Unemployment in the Eurozone is much higher than in the UK because unemployment benefit is much more generous. It is linked to the level of education and the last income. As economists say, much of unemployment is voluntary. In other words why would a highly educated person who lost a job look for a low-skilled low paid job for the sake of „nobility of work"when they can receive much more in the form of unemployment benefit.

It is not true that British industrial workers became the richest in the EU. One of the reasons why the UK is more attractive for foreign investors than continental European countries is that real wagesa are lower, trade unions are weaker and employees have less rights.

4. Atkinson wants to prove that there are countries which are not EU members that depend much more on trade with the EU than the UK. On page 84 he states that 66% of Switzerland's exports go to the EU and that only 9% of the UK's GDP is traded with the EU. What attracts the reader's attention is a striking difference between numbers 9 and 66. In fact the comparison is not plausible since it uses two different indicators, exports/GDP ratio and ratio of exports to certain area/total exports. A comparison which used the same indicators would show that the UK with 59% of its exports going to the EU is not far off Switzerland. Later Atkinson mentions this figure of 59%. However, he states that one third of these exports use EU ports such as Rotterdam to end up in non EU countries. He estimates that only 40% of the UK exports go to the EU. It is quite normal that Switzerland, although not an EU member, depends more on trade with the EU than the UK, which is an EU member. Small countries in general depend more on foreign trade than big countries. Their foreign trade/GDP ratio is much higher, while bigger countries are more self-sufficient. Switzerland is geographically surrounded by a thick wall of the EU countries and it is quite logical that its trade is oriented towards its neighbours (a trade pattern explained by the so called „The gravity theory").

5. Atkinson argues that the EU and especially the Euro have brought economic disaster to all the member countries. Empirical analysis, however shows that different countries have had a different experience within the EU. Some countries, like Greece, have experienced relative retardation in economic development. Before joining the EU in 1981 Greek GDP per capita, adjusted to the purchasing power was at 77% of the EU average. During the 1980's it fell to 62% and only rose

to 65% during the 1990's. On the other hand countries like Portugal, Spain and especially Ireland have benefitted a lot from the EU membership. Before joining the EEC in 1973 Ireland's GDP per capita, adjusted to the purchasing power, was at 64% of the EU average. It had risen to 70% at the beggining of the 1990's. Owing to a vigorous growth in the 1990's and staggering growth rates whihc sometimes reached a double digit at the turn of the century Ireland reached the EU average and caught up with the UK. Atkinson is right that the UK does not have a fair deal as the second largest contributor to the EU budget. If the UK's GDP is at the EU average, same as Ireland's GDP, then the UK should not be a net donor and Ireland a net recipient from the EU fund.

6. Atkinson claims that the vast majority of the EU citizens are essentially against the surrendering of national sovereignty to the European super-state. The only reason why referenda were successful is that the question at referenda was cleverly phrased and that voters were exposed to manipulation. But the art of manipulation is at the centre of parliamentary democracy. Success in parliamentary elections requires huge amounts of money and the support of powerful media. People vote not for the best political ideas, but for those which are best advertised. How many people have enough knowledge to figure out what best serves their interests? Only in the ancient democracies, where all free citizens were virtually members of parliament, did they directly influence a decision making process. On the other hand personal freedoms were restricted. For example, all men in Athens had to grow beard and women were not allowed to take more than three skirts when travelling. In the parliamentary democracy the influence of voters on the decision-making process is negligible. What makes a gist of parliamentary democracy is that personal freedoms are almost limitless.

7. Atkinson claims that the concept of united Europe is essentially German and Catholic. If the concept is Catholic this means that it is not undemocratic and unpopular. During my short stay in Slovakia in 1990 the most popular song was

an Italian entry and later the winner of the Eurovision song contest „*Tuto in sieme*"(Everything together). People told me that the message was so powerful that the song deserved the first place. A Polish entry to this year The Eurovision contest with its refrain „*Keine Grenze keine Fahnen*"(No borders no flags) proves that Polish people are in favour of a united Europe. It is true that Catholic nations might be more in favour of a united Europe due to the fact that the Catholic church organisation is international in its character. Protestant and Ortodox nations, whose church organisations are national in its character, might be more concerned with the preservation of their national identity and nation states.

8. Atkinson argues that both Mussolini and Hitler, who wanted to restore the German Roman empire, were socialists and Roman Catholics. Mussolini was a declared atheist and in a certain part of his life a socialist and with a socialist father, who named him after Benito Juarez, the Latin American socialist. He was actively involved in the Italian Socialist Party and regularly wrote for its newspaper *Lotta per la Liberta* (Struggle for Freedom). Disappointed by the lack of „class consciencesness"amongst the working class he turned fascist after the WWI. Hitler was for a six months a member of a communist-led workers council during the 19191 revolution. But right from the start he did not hide his hatred towards the left-wing movement. Today, however this piece of information is irrelevant since Pro-European political organisations are clustered around the political centre. Right-wing and left-wing parties are against a united Europe. First, because they are concerned for the future of nation states. Second, because they consider a united Europe as a project of big capital and multinational corporations.

But it is hard to call Hitler a Roman Catholic. The whole Nazi movement was anti-Christian in its nature. Nazis considered Christianity an alien body, a Jewish conspiracy whose aim was to undermine a vigorous German spirit and their right to rule the world. They returned to old German mithology and pagan rituals. When Hindenburg died Hitler made a speech in which he said that Hindenburg had entered Valhalla (a place where according to German mythology heroes settled after death). Had he been a Roman Catholic he would have most probably said that Hindenburg had been ressurected in heaven and found peace with God.

9. If the concept of a united Europe is German it should not be alien to the peoples of Eastern and Central Europe. They share many values with the German people, the education system and the foundation of the legal system are very similar and very different from the Anglo-Saxon education and legal system. Historical links, geographical proximity, trade, cultural and linguistic links (as Frederick Forsythe said in one of his novels many Yugoslavs speak some German, to Czechs, Slovaks, Hungarians and Poles it amounts to more than some) make it easier for Eastern and Central European countries to reconcile their system to the similar German than to the remote „American way of life".

10. Atkinson is especially subjective, emotionally charged, biased and ill informed when it comes to „the Yugolav affairs".

   a) Atkinson claims that the British government supported its fascist enemies, Slovaks, Croats, Bosnians and Slovenians against its anti-fascist Serb friends. This statement is superficial, unfounded and biased. In all the above mentioned nations, including Serbs, there were those who collaborated with the Nazis for different reasons. Slovaks and Croats who collaborated with the Nazis did it because the latter helped them to realise their historical dream, the establishment of an independent state. Slovenes and Serbs who collaborated with the Nazis did it to survive. Slovenes were in a particularly difficult situation since Hitler decided partly to resettle and partly to Germanise them and turn Slovenia into an eastern outpost of the Third Reich. As far as Serbs are concerned General Milan Nedic, who fought Germans in the WWI, collaborated with the Nazis not because he was a fascist, but because he wanted to save the Serbian nation from annihilation after

Hitler threatened to divide Serbia proper between Croatian *Ustashas*, Hungarians and Bulgarians. Atkinson completely overlooks historical context and is entirely biased.

b) On several occasions Atkinson stated that the Croatian army ethnically cleansed 300,000 Croatian Serbs with a full support from the Western countries. Atkinson most probably does not know that the Croatian army expelled 300,000 Serbs also with a full support of Serbian politicians outside Croatia. Milosevic and his cronies and puppets considered Krajina Serbs nothing more than to serve to fill-in. The deal was struck between Tudjman and Milosevic to resettle Krajina Serbs as well as Croats in Vojvodina in order to make more nationally homogenous territories. For that purpose Tudjman tried to encourage Croats in Vojvodina to ask for seccession from Serbia. However, Croats in Vojvodina had much wiser leaders than Krajina Serbs. Bela Tonkovic, the president of the main political organisation of Croats of Vojvodina did not bite the hook. He asserted that Croats from Vojvodina did not know a homeland other than Serbia and Yugoslavia and limited his ambitions to the restoration of cultural autonomy. Unlike Croats from Vojvodina, Krajina Serbs became the victims of manipulation. Jovan Raskovic, the founder of the Serbian Democratic Party in Croatia, a highly educated and modern politician, was aware that in all deals between Serbian and Croatian politicians Krajina would remain in Croatia. First, because it is geographically far from Serbia, second because it is poor and therefore economically of no interest for Serbia. This is why he wanted to make a deal with Tudjman to secure cultural autonomy and to negotiate teritorial autonomy for the Croatian Serbs. Milosevic did not like Raskovic because he could not manipulate him. After Draskovic died he was replaced by totally incompetent Milosevic's puppets, who did not realise that they were the objects of manipulation. When the Croatian army launched the attack in August 1995 there were no serious attempts to defend the teritory.

Military experts were sent from Belgrade to help organise withdrawal and not defence, although the balance of military power was far from clear. The Croatian army had 25 planes, Krajina Serbs 20. The whole Croatian army had 130,000 soldiers, Krajina Serbs 50,000. The leaders of Krajina Serbs blindly followed the instructions from Belgrade unaware that they had been betrayed a long time ago.

c) On several occasions Atkinson claims that Serbs had always made up at least 50% of the population of Kosovo before the WWII. According to the census of population in 1921, whose results were announced in the book „The Maps of our Divisions", published in Belgrade in 1988, Serbs made up the majority only in the Northern part of Kosovo and as far as towns are concerned in Kosovska Mitrovica. In all other parts of Kosovo including the major towns the Albanian population was in a majority. King Alexander was aware that a change in ethnic structure was needed when he stated that Istria was populated by Croats and Slovenes and that it was just a matter of time when it was going to join Yugoslavia. After 20 years of a deliberate policy of settling Serbs in Kosovo they made up 43% and Albanians 455 of the population of the province in 1941.

d) Atkinson claims that Croatian *Ustashas* killed 1 million Serbs and between 400,000 and 700,000 in Jasenovac. Atkinson is not aware that the number of war victims in Yugoslavia was deliberately inflated for decades. In 1946 Vladeta Vuckovic, then a student of Mathematics, later a university professor in the USA, got the task from the Yugoslav government to inflate the number of the war victims by using sophisticated statistical methods. The Yugoslav government needed as many victims as possible so that it could claim higher reparations from the West German government. Vuckovic came up with the figure of 1.6 million killed. As far as Jasenovac is concerned the official figures were 700,000 killed; 500,000 Serbs, 100,000 Jews and Gypsies and 100,000 antifascists.

Later research conducted by various Yugoslav historians (Dusan Biber, Ivo Lach, Btanko Miljus, Bogoljub Kocovic) has shown that around 200,000 people were killed in Jasenovac and around 1 million in the whole of Yugoslavia. The figure of 1 million Serbs killed only by *Ustashas* is unsubstantiated. Before the WWII Serbs made up 43.5% of the population of Bosnia and Herzegovina. After the WWII Serbs retained the relative majority of 41%. Had 1 million Serbs had been killed only by *Ustashas* it would have been impossible for them to retain the relative majority in Bosnia and Herzegovina after the WWII.

e) Atkinson claims that 30,000 civilians were killed when Germans bombed Belgrade on 6 April 1941. The official figure in the former Yugoslavia was that 10,000 people were killed, including 2,240 civilians. The greatest number of casualties I have come across was given in Tudjman's book „Croatia in Monarchist Yugoslavia". Tudjman estimates that 17,000 people were killed. But this includes civilians and soldiers who died in the fighting which followed the bombing. In 1941 Belgrade had 250,000 inhabitants. It would be impossible even for the *Luftwaffe*"to wipe out 12% of the population of the capital city just in one day. Again, as on previous occasions the figures are unchecked and based on hearsay.

f) There are also two minor mistakes in dates. On page 156:"1913-Albania was an artificial creation by Germany and Austria-Hungary". Albania was actually created on 28 November 1912 by Italy and Austro-Hungary. On page 163:"1974-Bosnian Moslems become a nation". Moslems were recognised as a separate nation in 1963 and appeared for the first time in the census of population in 1971.

In spite of these weaknesses the book is a valuable contribution to the literature on the European Union. Atkinson has raised well-founded concerns regarding the future of Europe. The concept of a united Europe has its advantages and disadvantages. What will prevail does not depend only on the nature of the project but also on the way it is implemented. At present the main drawback in the way the project is implemented is a lack of legitimacy. In numerous studies on the European Union it is mentioned that the European Parliament should be given legislative power. This would give the opportunity to peoples of the European Union to choose their representatives who will pass the laws in the same way as they do in their national elections. The idea of a confederative European state instead of federal, which would retain national sovereignty in matters vital for national interest, might be the way out of the current impasse. If the European Parliament is marginalised in the future the Orwellian prediction might easily become a reality.

Atkinson has a lot of reasons for his gloomy economic predictions for the Euroland. After the Euro replaced the national currencies its value dropped until the ECB in Frankfurt decided to prop up the currency with interventions on the exchange market. But more important is that other economic indicators such as growth rates were lower than in other developed countries and that unemployment was higher. Although high unemployment is partly voluntary because of generous unemployment benefits it should have been much lower considering fundamentally sound foundations of the world economy. Atkinson is right that this could be partly because unemployment (and possibly the growth rate) was not added to convergence criteria set as the conditions for adopting the Euro.

Atkinson is right that Germany is trying to assume the leading position in a united Europe and therefore to achieve peacefully what she failed to do in the two world wars. Considering the fact that the German economy is the largest in Europe there is nothing strange in this ambition. What matters is whether power is used with or without responsibility. The historical experience with Germany carrying power is not good and Atkinson is right that historical frustrations might again emerge.

Parts of the book in which Atkinson is not emotionally involved and biased and in which he sticks to objective analysis and well founded facts are masterly written. He shows erudition in economic, legal, political, historical and matters related to the philosophy of history. Being hostile to the whole project he does not give suggestions how to improve the functioning of the European Union and the Euroland. Therefore, his book is only a useful warning of what should have been done and what needs to be avoided if the whole project of a united Europe is to be successful.

Enver Redzic:"Bosnia and Herzegovina in the Second World War" Frank Cass, London-New York, 2006

The book 'Bosnia and Herzegovina in the Second World War' represent a detailed research of military activities and political developments in the country from 1941 until 1945. The author is a renowned scholar, who used a wide range of resources to provide information about complex developments in Bosnia and Herzegovina during the WW2. A lion's share of the work consists of the viewpoints of the primary participants. The book is therefore less a narrative of events in a chronological order or a military history but more a collection of perceptions and assessments. The protagonists inevitably saw events in a different light. In spite of this there is a significant overlap in their observation of the main issues, which helps to produce some sort of consensus on the main causes, developments and outcomes of the war.

There were five major participants in Bosnia and Herzegovina during the WW2; German and Italian occupiers, Ustasha, Chetniks, Muslim SS divisions and Communist-led Partisans. Each of these participants had their goals which could be analysed on the strategic and tactical level.

The Rome agreement on 18th April 1941 defined the roles of Germans and Italians in Bosnia and Herzegovina. Although Germans agreed that Italians should have a predominant political influence in the country they insisted to divide Bosnia and Herzegovina into the German and the Italian zone. The German zone comprised the most developed parts of the country. Germans wanted to have the control of the raw materials and manufacturing products in order to support their war efforts. On the tactical level they supported the Independent State of Croatia (NDH), with a vital military aid. Their view of Muslims was based on reports sent by Hermann von Neurbacher and Siegfried von Kasche. They considered Muslims unreliable and opportunistic. However, Hitler praised military prowess of Muslim soldiers recalling the memories of the WW1, when they fought in the Austro-Hungarian army. German considered Serbs their arch enemies. Hitler supported Pavelic's policy of intolerance towards the Serbs for the next 50 years. However, they were against Ustasha genocide policy towards the Serbs, blaming it for the uprising.

Italians wanted a political control of the entire Bosnia and Herzegovina. To achieve this they needed a support of at least a part of the native population. They chose Serbs as allies, whom they tried to protect from Ustasha terror. Later they collaborated with the Chetnics, supplying them with food, ammunition and weapons. They completely ignored the Muslims and despised the Croats, trying to undermine the 'sovereignty' of the NDH wherever and whenever they could.

Ustasha based their ideology on the teachings of Ante Starcevic and Eugen Kvaternik, according to which Bosnia and Herzegovina is a natural and historical part of the Croatian state. Ante Starcevic considered Muslims 'a purest stock of the Croatian nation' and Serbs in Croatia and Bosnia and Herzegovina Croats of the Orthodox faith. However, Ustasha ignored this part of Starcevic's teaching by acquiring a hostile attitude towards the Serbs, based on radicalism of the Croatian Party of Right. They flattered Muslims by calling them 'flowers of the Croatian nation'. They treated Serbs as their main enemy, wanting to purge the Croatian territory of them. To achieve this they planned to kill one third of Serbs, to convert one third to Catholicism and to expel one third to Serbia. On the tactical level Ustasha relied on German support, without whose military support NDH would have been unviable right from its inception. They disliked Italians, opposed to the formation of exclusively Muslim SS divisions and any autonomy of Bosnia and Herzegovina and from

1942 onwards occasionally entered into an unholy alliance with the Chetnics.

Although the Chetnic movement in Bosnia and Herzegovina was a great deal autonomous it shared a main strategic goal with its centre in Serbia. Political aims of the Chetnic movement were defined at the congress in a village Ba in Western Serbia from 25 to 28 January 1944. A memorandum drawn up at the congress envisaged expansionist Serbia and expansionist Yugoslavia. After the war Yugoslavia will be a federation consisted of three units; Serbia, Croatia and Slovenia. A Serbian federation will include Macedonia, Montenegro, Bosnia and Herzegovina and large parts of Slavonia and Dalmatia. The plan envisaged expansionist Yugoslavia which will incorporate all areas of the neighbouring countries were Serbs, Croats and Slovenes live. Other Slav nations (Bosnian Muslims, Green Montenegrins and Macedonians) will be ignored. In Yugoslavia there will be no place for national minorities. The country will be a constitutional and parliamentary monarchy ruled by the Karadjordjevic dynasty. The memorandum suggested a democratic order with a multiparty political system, although some extremist delegates at the congress advocated several years of Chetnic dictatorship after the war.

At the tactical level Chetnics' aim was to protect Serbs from genocide. By doing this they committed atrocities against Muslims and Croats, justifying it as a revenge for Ustasha terror. Their main allies were Italians. Germans refused co-operation with the Chetnics before Italy capitulated, fearing that at a first opportunity Chetnics will turn against them and help the Allies. They occasionally made agreements with Ustasha, initiated by the occupiers. Chetnics wanted to destroy Muslims and committed a genocide against them in 1941 and 1942. Some Chetnic leaders, such as Dobrosav Jevdjevic, suggested a more tolerant attitude towards Muslims. They claimed that most of Muslims had not committed crimes against Serbs and suggested the creation of Muslim Chetnic units. This line was fully supported by Draza Mihajlovic, who sent his representative Mustafa Mulalic to spread Chetnic propaganda among Muslims. However, after Chetnic atrocities Muslim response was poor. Chetnics were the only participant who collaborated with Partisans, with whom they shared a strategic goal of a restoration of Yugoslavia, albeit on different political and ideological grounds.

At the beginning of the war Muslims were divided into three factions regarding policies in Bosnia and Herzegovina. The first and the smallest one supported NDH government and Ustasha. The second one, slightly bigger, supported the Partisan movement. The third, the largest one was in a favour of autonomy of Bosnia and Herzegovina within NDH (in this attempt Muslims were supported by many Serbs) or an independent state of Bosnia and Herzegovina under the German protectorate. In 1943 two Muslim SS divisions were formed in order to back up militarily autonomist tendencies. Germans welcomed the creation of Muslim SS divisions so that they could release some forces from the Balkans and send them to the other fronts. The divisions consisted of 60% Muslims, some Albanians and almost 40% Germans. The SS Muslim divisions had a little success for two reasons; first, the conscription was forceful and second their soldiers terrorised Serb civilians. As a result moral was low and desertion frequent. Many members of the divisions who deserted joined the Partisans.

Some books about WW2 in Yugoslavia, written in the West, state that Chetnics had started their resistance against the fascist occupiers on the 9th May 1941 while Communist-led Partisans were not involved before 22nd June when Germany attacked the Soviet Union. The author claims that in April and May 1941 CPY (Communist Party of Yugoslavia) issued declarations inviting the citizens of the country regardless of their nation, religion or political conviction to rise against the fascist oppressors, but that organised uprising did not start long after 22nd of June. Even 27th July, which was officially regarded in Communist Yugoslavia as a day of uprising in Bosnia and Herzegovina, was more the results of a spontaneous revolt than organised action with no clear distinction between Chetnic and Partisan involvement. This might lead to the conclusion that the beginning of the WW2 caught CPY unprepared.

The main strategic goals of the Communist-led partisan movement were defined at the session of ZAVNOJ (Anti-fascist Council of the National Liberation of Yugoslavia) held at the end of November 1943 in Jajce. Documents released at the session envisaged a new Yugoslavia as a democratic federation consisted of six republics; Bosnia and Herzegovina, Croatia, Macedonia, Montenegro, Serbia and Slovenia. The documents stated that the new country would respect inviolability of private property and freedom of speech, religion and political organisation. None of the documents, however, mentioned that the future country would become a communist dictatorship, albeit the softest one in the whole of the Communist world.

On the tactical level the Partisan movement faced many difficulties which stemmed from the complex national, religious and political situation in Bosnia and Herzegovina as well as from the dogmatic Stalinist approach, which at the beginning of the war was very often detached from reality. Partisans collaborated with the Chetnics in 1941 and 1942. As the war progressed this coalition broke up so that Partisans found themselves fighting all the other major participants. In spite of this their ranks swelled, especially after 1943, and they emerged victorious at the end of the war. The author explains a Partisan military victory by the fact that they offered the most satisfactory solution to the national question in Bosnia and Herzegovina and Yugoslavia.

The book does not analyse external factors which contributed to the success of the Partisan movement. There is only one sentence which states that the Partisan movement received an enormous boost when the Allies in 1943 Tehran conference decide to support them instead of Chetnics.

The author joined the Partisans during the WW2 and attended key wartime Partisan political councils. He wrote 15 books regarding nationality issues in Yugoslavia and Bosnia and Herzegovina, most of them during the communist period. However, in this book he does not follow the official communist line according to which the Partisan struggle had a dual character (national liberation and social revolution). Alleged superiority of the communist ideology, a part of the official explanation of the Partisans success during the communist period, was never mentioned in the book. The book reveals two details which were omitted in a romanticized official historiography; The first one that the Partisans negotiated a ceasefire with Germans in Zagreb in March 1943; The second one that the Partisan soldiers were also involved in plundering and looting, although on a smaller scale than Ustasha and Chetnics.

The explanation which finds the main reason for Partisans' success in its national policy is the plausible one when compared with the national policies of the other two domestic movements.

Ustasha national policy failed to recognise that NDH was a multinational state with barely 50% of Croats. They pursued a policy of genocide towards Serbs, who made up 30% of the population of the NDH and who would have been treated in any normal state as a constituent nation. They alienated Muslims by treating them as Croats of the Islamic faith. As the war progressed more Croats became disillusioned with NDH so that support for the Ustasha among them stood at 2% in 1943. Chetnic national policy might have appealed to a large number of Serbs and probably to Slovenes. However, it was totally unacceptable to Croats, Muslims, Montenegrins and Macedonians, not to mention national minorities. A national policy of the Partisan movement, which envisaged a future Yugoslav federation in which Bosnia and Herzegovina will be one of the six republics with equal rights for its three constituent nations had a strong appeal to Croats and especially Muslims, who joined the Partisan movement in droves after 1943. Serbs in Bosnia and Herzegovina were also satisfied with this solution. Owing to a widespread participation in the Partisan movement they considered themselves the pillars of the Bosnian statehood within the new Yugoslav federation.

The book 'Bosnia and Herzegovina in the Second World War' deals with the topic widely explored and researched. What distinguishes it from research done by other authors is the original approach in which viewpoints of all the participants are presented and analysed. This is why this book represents an extremely interesting read.

Marko Attila Hoare: "The Bosnian Muslims in the Second World War: A History", Hurst & Company, London 2013

Marko Attila Hoare's *The Bosnian Muslims in the Second World War* follows on his book *Genocide and Resistance in Hitler's Bosnia*. Unlike the previous work, this book is more specific in topic and covers the period from 1941 until 1950.

Through a galore of facts and syntagms which can befuddle even natives of the land, such as pro-Chetnik Partisans, pro-Partisan Chetniks, Croatian Communists, Croatian non-Communist Partisans, Muslim Communist Partisans, Muslim non-Communist Partisans, Muslim Ustashasa, Muslim Chetniks, Croatian Green Cadre soldiers, Croatian members of Handschar division, through a myriad of relations, fickle allegiances and frequently swapping sides of war participants, skilfully leads us to the theme of his book.

In the beginning of the war Partisan leadership was multi-ethnic, while rank and file consisted predominantly of Serb peasants escaping from and fighting against Ustasha genocide. Partisan leadership was aware that in order to win the war they had to conquer cities and towns where Muslims made up an absolute majority. Therefore, winning Muslims' support became essential in an overall struggle with German and Italian invaders and their domestic collaborators.

Initially, a majority of Muslims viewed the new Croatian puppet state, i.e. the NDH, with hope that their position would improve compared to the one they had in the Kingdom of Yugoslavia and with loyalty to the new regime. The most ardent supporters of the new state were former members of the Muslim branch of the HSS, Hakija Hadzic, Ademaga Mesic and Alija Suljak. They removed from political life Muslim notables, who were leaders of the JMO and who were suspicious of the new regime and particularly leaders of the pro-Serb cultural society Gajret.

A several months after the establishment of the NDH a vast majority of Muslims became disillusioned in the new state. Disappointment with the new regime stemmed from three causes:Firstly, the NDH leadership wanted to obliterate borders between Bosnia and Herzegovina and Croatia, denying any peculiarity to the former. Protests of some politicians of all the three main ethnic groups and requests for autonomy for Bosnia and Herzegovina within the NDH ended up with harsh repression from the authority; arrests of Bosnian Muslims and Bosnian Croat protesters and murder of three Bosnian Serb politicians.

Secondly, the NDH leaders wanted forcibly to assimilate Bosnian Muslims into a Croatian nation with obsequious declarations that the former were the purest stock of the Croatian nation since they did not intermingle with other races while Croats in Croatia had mixed with Germans, Hungarians and Italians. Thirdly, Muslims bore the brunt of Chetniks' and sometimes even Partisans' retaliation for Ustasha atrocities against Serb civilians, and the NDH authorities were either unwilling or unable to protect them. As a result Muslims' attitude became increasingly anti-Ustasha and pro-German.

Muslim notables hoped that they would get support from Germans in their desire to establish an autonomous Bosnia and Herzegovina and even an independent state. These efforts culminated in formation of the 13th SS Handschar division, a so called Himmler's division, and memorandum to Hitler. In a memorandum to Hitler, Muslim notables asked him to support the establishment of an independent Bosnia and Herzegovina as a German protectorate. They suggested the secession of border land territories to neighbouring countries and exchange of population in order to achieve a rump Bosnia and Herzegovina with a Muslim majority.

Partisan leadership shared views of an autonomous Bosnia and Herzegovina with Muslim notables. Their slogans were full of Bosnian patriotism whose aim was to gather all the three main Bosnian ethnic groups. They had in mind a Bosnian statehood within a new Yugoslav federation, although the words federation and Yugoslavia were not mentioned before 1943. However, Muslim masses did not join the Partisan movement in large numbers before 1943 fearing Ustasha and German reprisals.

Muslims were soon disappointed in the Germans for two reasons. First, Hitler never paid much attention to the idea of autonomous Bosnia and Herzegovina. Second, Muslim youth were forcibly recruited to 13th SS Handschar division and sent to various fronts abroad including the Eastern front, while they expected to stay at home and defend Muslim villages from Chetniks and to a lesser degree from Ustashas. This disappointment culminated in a mutiny in Villefranche-de-Rouergue in 1943. In the absence of soldiers of this division, various local militias were formed in Muslim villages to protect civilians. They increasingly collaborated with the NOP.

A decisive moment came in 1943 with two very important events; the capitulation of Italy on 8 September and the first session of a communist assembly of Bosnia and Herzegovina, ZAVNOBIH, on 25th November. During the first two years of the war Chetniks were the minions of the Italians who armed them and supported them. After Italy capitulated, the Germans took over the role of Chetnik supporters. In order to motivate them for all-out war with the Partisans, the Germans promised the creation of the Great Serbian Federation, which would include the Serbia proper, Sanjak, Montenegro, and East Bosnia. This caused a panic among Muslims and Bosnian Croats. At the same time Bosnian statehood was cemented at the first session of the ZAVNOBIH held in Mrkonjic Grad. These two events prompted a massive influx of Muslims and to a lesser degree Bosnian Croats into the Partisan movement.

In 1944 the Ustashas and especially the Chetniks toned down their militant nationalism in order to attract Muslims to their ranks. In the congress at village Ba in Western Serbia, held in January 1944, Zivko Topalovic, one of the founders of the KPJ, advocated the creation of Bosnia and Herzegovina as the fourth federal unit in future Yugoslavia. However, he was a single voice in the sea of Great Serbian sentiments spearheaded by Dragisa Vasic and especially Stevan

Moljevic, who could see his Bosanska Krajina nowhere but in Greater Serbia.

Draza Mihailovic tried to court Muslims by promising them that after the war Sarajevo would become an Islamic centre of Europe. This promise sounded rather hollow after atrocities which Chetniks committed against Muslim civilian population and had a very limited appeal.

Marko Attila Hoare discusses in length various proposals for a Bosnian coat of arms and flag after the war. At the end it was decided that the flag would be red in colour, symbolising the blood of all Bosnian citizens spilt in struggle for freedom. In the background there was a picture of the town Jajce. This was supposed to link the present with the past; the town which was the seat of the first session of ZAVNOJ, and at the same time the seat of them medieval Bosnian kings.

An especially interesting chapter from the legal point of view is the one entitled:" Did Bosnia and Herzegovina have the right to secede from Yugoslavia?" In this chapter Marko Attila Hoare juxtaposes two very important issues:1. Federation versus confederation, and 2. A right of republics for self-determination including secession versus the right of peoples for self-determination including secession.

The first important issue requires a clarification of differences between federation and confederation. In federation the original sovereignty belongs to the federal state. Federal state devolves to constituent units as much power as it wants. In practical terms this means that federal units, states, republics etc. can pass their constitutions and laws if they do not contravene federal constitution and federal laws. In confederation the original sovereignty lies with the states, which pass on to confederative bodies as many powers as they want. For the beginning these powers usually include monetary policy, customs union, foreign trade, foreign affairs and army.

Hoare lucidly points at the place which reveals the ambiguity of the legal arrangements in the new Yugoslav state. On the page 311 he quotes a prominent Bosnian politician Dusko Sakota:

> *"Our federation was established in order to resolve the national question. Thus, that the principle of the Federation has been consistently realised is manifested in the fact that the*

People's Republics are sovereign states. They are limited only in the rights that the peoples of Yugoslavia have, through their own decision, transferred to the Federative People's Republic of Yugoslavia. The transfer of these rights was necessary to achieve economic and political co-operation and the reciprocal assistance of the peoples' republics; their common defence, state security and independence; and with a goal of a unified democratic manner of state and social order of all the People's Republics in the composition of the FNRJ. Other than these most important affairs of importance to all the peoples, exercised through the Federal government in the general interest, the People's Republics exercise their government independently, maintaining their sovereignty."

This would suggest a confederative model of the new Yugoslav state.

A paragraph on page 313 reads:

... *"The Commission for the Preparation of the Draft Constitution had consulted senior officials of the Yugoslav government responsible for constitutional affairs to ensure that the Bosnian constitution would be in keeping with the Yugoslav Constitution; these officials submitted their last set of corrections, all of them fairly minor, to the People Government on 7th November."*

This would suggest a federative model of the new Yugoslav state.

The other issue, another source of ambiguity, became increasingly relevant before and during the Wars for Yugoslav Succession, waged from 1991 until 1995. Croats and Muslims understood that the republics had the right for self-determination including secession. Serbs, on the other hand, interpreted the legal arrangements in Yugoslavia, as if the peoples had the right for self-determination including secession. With this they assumed that the territories with a Serb majority had the right to secede from Croatia and Bosnia and Herzegovina and join Serbia.

The book is a result of many years of thorough and meticulous research. The best proof of the time the research took is the fact that the first interview was held with Zvonko Vonta Ivanovic on 9 June 1996 and the last one with Mirko Dubajic on 6 October 2000.

The book has more than 1,600 footnotes. A bibliography is equally impressive, containing more than 400 sources. They are classified in the following groups:1. Archives, 2. Published documents, 3. Newspapers and journals-historical, 4. Historical texts, 5. Autobiographies, diaries, eyewitness accounts and works of fiction, and 6. Secondary sources. As in his previous books Marko Attila Hoare consulted more resources in Bosnian/Serb-Croat than in English. One source is in Italian.

The Bosnian Muslims in the Second World War represents a brilliant political, historical and to a lesser extent legal analysis. I warmly and with pleasure recommend it to readers.

Marin Vetma: "Father's pledge – 1944". Latrobe Bookbinding, 2004

The book *Father's pledge – 1944* is mainly a collection of the author's memoirs and articles written in various newspapers and journals. It also contains correspondence between Yugoslav intellectuals living abroad and interviews with the Partisan general Milan Basta, and the famous social scientist and dissident of the Yugoslav communist period, Mihajlo Mihajlov.

It consists of three parts: The first part is entitled *Memoirs*, the second *New Millenium – Quo Vadis* and the third part *O Tempora o Mores*.

The first part is the author's recollection of events in Split region following the beginning of the war and collapse of Yugoslavia in 1941. In a general atmosphere of chaos, anarchy, fear and persecution by *Ustasha* authorities several prominent citizens of Split asked the Italians for help and protection. The Italians seized the opportunity to annex Dalmatia, leaving only the islands of Brac and Hvar to the NDH (Independent state of Croatia). Life under the Italian occupation was one of relative security, although fraught with tension and hatred towards the occupier. When Italy capitulated in 1943 chaos and fear returned. Marin Vetma was 20 years old and in the final year of a classical grammar school. He was "loved" and at the same time suspected by all armies: the Ustashas, Chetniks, Italians and Partisans who wanted to recruit him. Fleeing an environment of constant danger Marin Vetma ended up in Serbia in 1944, where he reluctantly joined the Serbian *Volunteers*. In 1945, after going through a real Calvary in Serbia he found himself in Slovenia and luckily escaped to Italy. Luckily, for those who withdrew to Austria were returned by the Allies to Slovenia where they were massacred by Tito's Partisans. The unlucky ones naively trusted an honourable word by a British officer, who believed and promised that they were going to Italy, forgetting or not knowing the main dictum, which has characterised British foreign policy for centuries:"There are no permanent friends there are only permanent interests". Marin Vetma spent two years in Italy in POW camps, under unpleasant living conditions. In 1948 he moved to Germany, his only wish being to leave Europe as soon as possible. After a series of interrogations he was released and embarked on a 40 day trip to Australia. In his new homeland, after many years of hardship and problems he eventually found peace and happiness in family life. The first part finishes with an extract from the book *Kocevje – Tito's Bloodiest Crime*, by Borivoje M. Karapandzic, in which a massacre of 28,000 anti-communist fighters is described.

The second part entitled *New Millenium – Quo Vadis* deals with a current crisis of Civilisation in which a technological progress is accompanied by a lack of moral values. Marin Vetma points out the hypocrisy of the world rulers, who allegedly in the name of democracy and freedom committed horrible atrocities. He explains tragic events in the last decade of the XX century and the beginning of the XXI century by the break-up of family as the nucleus of society. This behaviour of the world rulers and their counterparts in the former Yugoslavia is contrasted by numerous examples of individuals who sacrificed their lives to help other people and who in the most difficult conditions did not abandon their moral principles and values.

The third part entitled *O Tempora o Mores* deals with the destruction of Yugoslavia in 1991. The behaviour of politicians and so called intellectuals, very often communist converts, who worked in the interest of foreign countries is compared with the similar behaviour of the Croatian upper class in the past, who sold the country's independence for the sake of their own power and greed. This is contrasted with the enthusiastic and idealistic work of the bearers of the Yugoslav idea in Croatia and Serbia.

The book could have been better structured. For example, the extract from the book *Kocevje – Tito's bloodiest Crime*, would have fitted better in the third part of the book. The beginning and the end of the second part, dealing with the crisis of Civilisation could have been placed together. The end of the book, written in Serbo-Croat, could have been either a separate part or appendix.

Otherwise, the context of the book is excellent. The book is implicitly written as a thesis; a tragedy of the Vetma family in a wider context of the Yugoslav and European tragedy. And then again the second catastrophe of the South Slavs in a wider context of what seems to be incurable malaise of Western Civilisation.

The tragedy of the Vetma family reflects all senselessness and madness of ideological conflicts and wars in general. Marin's brother was killed as a Partisan in 1942. Marin, whose only ambition was to lead a peaceful life and get educated, had to flee his country as "an enemy of the people". Marin's father was arrested and tortured by the Germans, Italians and twice by Partisans who killed him in 1944, although he saved the life of a Communist who worked with him.

The book is full of useful information. Lives, actions and destines of prominent and less known figures in the Split region before, during and after WWII are described in detail. Also the political and military situation in Serbia and in Slovenia in 1945 is explained meticulously and accurately. Particularly impressive is the part of the book which deals with the history of the Illyrian movement and the Yugoslav idea in Croatia.

Two very interesting details are described in the book. One is more well-known and is related to the trial of Bishop Alojzije Stepinac. Stepinac would have been acquitted if he had bowed to Communist pressure to establish an independent Croatian Catholic Church. The other one is less known and is related to the capture of Krunoslav Draganovic. The Communist authorities did not want to try Draganovic since they needed him as a trump card in negotiations with the Vatican. After the negotiations had been completed Tito (excommunicated and atheist) had added another title to the already long list-an honorary dean of the Catholic Church.

Jack Saltman:'KURT WALDHEIM'-A Case to Answer?, Robson Books in association with Channel Four Television Company, London 1988

The book deals with one of the most publicised events in the second half of the 1980's, the allegations that a former General Secretary of the United Nations and at the time a president of Austria, Kurt Waldheim, was involved in war crimes in Greece and Yugoslavia during WWII. The accusations of Waldheim's participation in war crimes were serious to the extent that Americans put him on the *'Watch List'*, banning him from entering the USA. There was a growing pressure on Waldheim to resign his post as an Austrian president. In Austria initial reaction was an increase in Waldheim's popularity to 70%. However, when some evidence was produced support for him slumped to 46%. In Yugoslavia there were intense talks on the case. Rumours were spread that Yugoslavia put Waldheim on the list of war criminals in 1947. This detail is not mentioned in the book. Many Yugoslavs claimed that Waldheim had to undertake a compulsory military service in the *Wehrmacht* in the same way most of us had to serve *The Yugoslav People's Army*. On the other hand, there were those who argued that most of Germans and Austrians were conscripted in the *Wehrmacht* and that they have never been linked to any war crimes. In other words, where there is a smoke there is a fire.

Attracted by the controversy of the 'Waldheim case' Jack Saltman decided to undertake a task of four-hour Anglo-American TV inquiry, a unique programme in which five eminent judges of different nationalities would pass an informal verdict whether Waldheim had 'a case to answer'. The evidence would be presented by Allan Ryan, former US Justice Department Special Prosecutor and challenged by Lord Rawlinson, the former UK Attorney General.

Saltman and his team put an enormous effort in organising the programme. They travelled extensively, mainly to Yugoslavia, Greece and West Germany, but also to other countries such as Sweden and Switzerland to find judges from neutral countries.

The first part of the book entitled **'Production'** talks about difficulties the team encountered in their search for top historians, researches, translators, judges, and witnesses. More than half a dozen countries were visited by top historians and researches who investigated 29 archives and collected over 8000 pages of relevant documents. More than 250 people were interviewed. They included Waldheim's colleagues, former soldiers and officers of the *Wehrmacht*, Yugoslav, Greek and Greek Jewish civilians, British and Italian POW and expert witnesses. The most difficult and nerve-wrecking job was to find five judges from different countries. Some judges, who initially accepted the offer, later changed their mind. Eventually, persistence of the team paid off and two days before the recording of the programme took place five judges met as a group for the first time. They included Sir Frederick Lawton from the UK, Gustav Petren from Sweden, A. Gordon Cooper from Canada, Shirley Hufstedler from the USA and Walter Hubner from West Germany.

The second part of the book, entitled **'The Commission of Inquiry'**, sets the charges against Waldheim and than follows extracts or sometimes verbatim testimony taken down directly from witnesses or through the simultaneous translations given during the days of the inquiry. The charges against Waldheim were as follows:

Charge 1: War crimes committed in Yugoslavia with *Kampfgruppe Bader* in connection with the massacre and deportation of prisoners, including the civilian and partisan population, and the indiscriminate burning of villages.

Charge 2: War crimes committed with *Kampfgruppe West Bosnia* in connection with the massacre and deportation of prisoners during operations in the Kozara region of Yugoslavia. The aim of these operations was to destroy the partisans illegally and to terrorise civilians.

Charge 3: War crimes committed while in Athens, in connection with the indiscriminate killing of Greek civilians, and with the deportation of Italian prisoners-of-war following Italy's surrender to the Allies.

Charge 4: War crimes committed while in Arslaki/Salonika, in connection with the deportation of Jews from Crete, Corfu and Rhodes; and in connection with the capture, interrogation and subsequent execution of various commandos (British, Greek and others), following Hitler's illegal order of 18 October 1942 with reference to captured commandos.

The grounds for these charges are based on the fact that one does not need to be physically involved in killings to be accused for war crimes. A *degree of complicity* is enough to accuse someone for war crimes, especially if one new that killing and other acts were illegal from the point of view of the international law. An excuse' I just followed the orders', very often heard during the *Nuremberg trial* is not sufficient to exonerate someone from war crimes accusations. A testimony of 38 witnesses in the programme had the aim of establishing whether Kurt Waldheim, who served as a liaison officer, was in any way responsible for the already mentioned war crimes and was he in any way in a position to prevent them from happening.

The answer to this question could have been obtained not from civilians, but from Waldheim's colleagues in the *Wehrmacht and British and Italian POW*. Most of Waldheim colleagues claimed that he had only produced documents and reports and had acted as an interpreter and that had been neither responsible nor had had any knowledge of deportations and killings. The situation was complicated by the fact that some of Waldheim colleagues, who apparently liked him, talked highly of him and praised not only his intellectual, but also moral and human qualities. A minority of his colleagues, however, disliked him and claimed that Waldheim, belonging to a counterintelligence department Ic must have had a full knowledge of all operations undertaken by the *Wehrmacht*. A further complication was introduced by a testimony of Bruce Ogilvie, a British officer who was captured by the Germans and who claimed that Waldheim had saved his life. On the other hand he did not do anything to prevent killings of thousands of innocent civilians in Yugoslavia and Greece. This is contrasted with the event in which an ordinary Italian soldier *Pompeo de Poli*, when ordered to the firing squad to kill innocent civilians at Cajnice (a small town in Eastern Bosnia) said to his commanding officer:' I am not going to do that'. The Italian soldier did not suffer any punishment for his disobedience.

In this respect it is worth mentioning a testimony of Waldheim's predecessor in the Ic department, Dr Werner Schollen. He claims that Waldheim was critical of Nazis and that was probably an anti-Nazi. He also claims that Waldheim was an Austrian, proud of his country's historical heritage and that was looking down upon the races which lived in the Balkans.

Several questions arise from the above mentioned evidence. First, did Waldheim think that it was worth saving a life of a British officer and not thousands of civilians who belonged to the races he disliked? Or was an operation of hiding the identity of a British officer risk-less in comparison with an open attempt to save civilians? Would such an act of decency and humanity been followed by the replacement of a relatively cosy office job,(with frequent and long study leave absences), with horrors of the Eastern Front – the high price Waldheim was not willing to pay? Although Italians were not soft as an occupier, they were not match to brutality and cruelty of the Germans. In other words it was easier to be disobedient in the Italian Army than in the *Wehrmacht*. Especially that Hitler's illegal order of 18th October 1942 regarding a treatment of POW and civilians did not have a counterpart in the Italian Army.

Saltman mentioned that as a candidate for the post of the General Secretary of the United Nations Waldheim was a Soviet Union's favourite. Not being elaborated in the book this fact raises two questions. First, did the Soviet Union prefer someone from neutral Austria to a candidate who would pursue American interests? Or did the Soviets have an evidence against Waldheim and used it as a weapon to increase their weight in the United Nations? The same question could apply to Yugoslavia. Did Yugoslavia play the same game? It was conspicuous that Yugoslavia significantly increased its influence in the United Nations in the 1970's when Waldheim was at the top of that institution.

Without a final judgement of the TV jury and without any conclusions the book raises more questions than it gives answers. Another feature, which usually distinguishes books written by journalists from those written by researchers, is a lack of references. Only once, during a visit to Yugoslavia, Saltman mentioned a book on Waldheim written by Danko Vasovich. In spite of these drawbacks the book is a valid contribution to the topic and represents a very interesting read.

Robert Bideleux & Ian Jeffries:'The Balkans-A Post-Communist History'. Routledge, London, 2006

As the title and the number of pages suggest the book is an extensive and detailed analysis of the events which occurred in the Balkan countries after the fall of communism. The introduction and the conclusion are as important as the main body of the book. In the introduction the authors focus on the major problems which have haunted the Balkan countries throughout their history. In the conclusion they suggest somewhat unconventional solutions as how to overcome the current problems in the Balkan countries.

The authors refuse to define the Balkans in cultural terms in order to avoid the well known stereotypes. One stereotype they tackle is that mentalities, mindsets and attitudes of the Balkan people make them sub-European and inferior to their West European 'cousins'. The Balkans is rather a micro-cosmos of Europe. Although horrendous crimes against humanity were committed in the wars for the Yugoslav succession during the 1990's they are dwarfed by atrocities which took place in the Western Europe since the Middle Age. In their arrogance and with a high opinion of themselves Europeans in general often forget that Europe has been the most racist, the most xenophobic and the most bigoted part of the world.

Another stereotype tackled in the book is that the Balkan peoples are disadvantage because they are predominantly Christian Orthodox and Muslims and do not belong to the 'Latin West', which makes them less suitable for 'civilization'. The authors prove that many countries which belong to the 'Latin West', such as Croatia, Spain and Portugal found it difficult in recent history to establish a civil society based on the rule of law, respect for human rights and the rights for ethnic minorities. In that respect predominantly Christian Orthodox Greece and largely Muslim Turkey fare better.

A major obstacle for a successful transition to a modern society in the Balkans, according to the authors, lie in vertical power structure, vertical power relations, ethnic collectivism and clientilism. This is the legacy of Byzantine, Ottoman, nationalist and Communist rule. The best way to overcome these problems would be a fast acceptance into the European membership. A promise of the EU membership has already had a positive effect on the Balkan countries. They are more advanced in the transition process than the successor states of the former Soviet Union. The authors emphasize the importance of the requirements the European Commission set in the 'Copenhagen criteria', which stipulated 'stability of institutions guaranteeing democracy, the rule of law, human rights and respect for and protection of minorities, the existence of the functioning market economy as well as the capacity to cope with competitive pressure and market forces within the Union'. Equally important are regulations set in 'Madrid criteria, which stipulated that new members must posses the administrative-cum-judicial capacity to implement and comply with the obligations of membership (primarily the 93,000 pages of EU legislation, the *acquis communautaire*).

The authors are ardent advocates of the fast membership of the Balkan countries in the European Union since inter-communal conflicts and ethnic collectivism cannot be resolved within a narrow framework of a sovereign nation-state. They put their argument succinctly in the following statement:'The emerging supranational cosmopolitan legal order of the EU is consummating the shift from an 'old Europe 'of often primordial 'vertical' power relations and power structures, to a 'new Europe' based on the 'horizontally structured' ties of civil association and rule of law, which are the *sine qua non* of any truly *liberal* democracy and *liberal* capitalism. It is in this regard that both the requirements and the consequences of EU membership can do most to transform the Balkan polities, by fostering 'horizontally structured' civil societies and civil economics based on the rule of law, equal civil rights for all permanent residents, and the equality of all individuals before the law, for the first time after more than 2,000 years of unbroken 'verticality of power'.

The main body of the book consists of a country-by-country analysis of the contemporary history of each of the Balkan states:Albania, Bulgaria, Romania, Croatia, Serbia, Bosnia and Herzegovina, Macedonia, Montenegro and Kosovo. Greece and Slovenia are not included in the book. Greece because she has not experienced the Communist rule. Slovenia because it has more in common with Central and West European countries in terms of the standard of living, life style, attitudes and power structures than with the Balkan countries.

A survey of each and every state starts with a lengthy introductory profile of a country. It includes major geographic data, racial and ethnic composition of population, political, military, economic, legal and cultural history before the fall of communism. A post-communist history is analysed in a chronological order. Presidential and parliamentary elections in each and every country are researched in a great detail. This is followed by corresponding analysis of economic, political, legal and social changes. The conclusion of the analysis is that there is a little space for complacency in the Balkan countries. Currently, most of them experience high levels of poverty, unemployment, increasing income and wealth inequalities, corruption and unabated ethnic tensions. The authors reinforce their stance on a fast admission of the Balkan countries to the European Union. This time they put forward economic arguments. Currently, European structural funds are insufficient to resolve all the above mentioned economic problems. Only a vigorous flow of FDI (foreign direct investment) can radically reshape economies of the Balkan countries. The authors use experience of Spain and Portugal after their admission to the European Union to corroborate the link between a membership in the organization and the flow of FDI. They admit that this means a partial loss of national sovereignty and a submission to an undemocratic procedure within the EU. However, they state that this is the inevitable opportunity cost which will be far exceeded by the benefits which the membership in the EU offers.

The book is a crown of more than 30 years of research. The authors espouse admiring erudition in various fields: geography, ethnology, law, politics, economics, political, military and cultural history. A bibliography is equally impressive, as is expected in such a monumental piece of work. It has more than 400 sources. Although most of them are in English, sources in French, Italian, Portuguese, Romanian and Russian language are also used. The book is a must read for everyone interested in the region. It is therefore warmly recommended to readers.

PART TWO
POLITICS

Alija Izetbegovi:"Inescapable Questions – Autobiographical Notes" The Islamic Foundation, Leicester, England, 2003, pp 550,

The book **'Inescapable Questions – Autobiographical Notes '**is an autobiography of Alija Izetbegovic, a former President of Bosnia and Herzegovina and SDA (The Party of Democratic Action). It reveals a turbulent and remarkable life of a person who could be dubbed both *l'homme d'action'* and *'l'homme des idees'*. *L'homme d'action'* because of his political activity which spans more than a half century with three most important periods; two imprisonments by the communist authorities in 1946 and 1983 and the victory in the first elections in 1990, followed by the Bosnia and Herzegovina declaration of independence and war. *'L'homme des idees'* because of his scholarly and philosophical ideas espoused in his books 'The Islamic Declaration', 'Islam between East and West' and many speeches, lectures and interviews.

The book consists of an introduction, eight chapters and appendixes. The introduction is entitled' A Short History of Bosnia and Herzegovina 'and is based on the Noel Malcolm's book 'Bosnia – A Short History'. The chapters of the book are entitled:1. Youth and First Imprisonment, 2. The Sarajevo Trial, 3. Founding the Party and an Attempt to Reconstruct Yugoslavia, 4. War Diary, 5. Srebrenica, 6. War and Jaw, 7. Dayton Diary and 8. After Dayton. Appendices contain various lectures, interviews and General Divjak's letter.

The longest part of Alija Izetbegovic's life was described in the first two chapters of the book. They reveal several interesting, less known details. His paternal grandfather comes from Belgrade. He moved to Bosnia with his family in 1868, the year when Muslims left Serbia. He settled near Bosanski Samac, a town which did not exist at the time. Alija Izetbegovic was born in Bosanski Samac in 1925. His maternal grandmother was Turk. After his father's merchant company went bankrupt Alija Izetbegovic moved to Sarajevo, where he received primary and part of secondary education before the WWII. His mother was a devout woman, which had a decisive influence on his religious upbringing and world view. From 1939 to 1941 Izetbegovic intensively befriended communists. This is the only period in his life when he started doubting his religious affiliations. During the WWII he dodged all conscriptions and managed to complete secondary education in 1943. In 1946 he was arrested and sentenced to several years of imprisonment together with other so called Young Muslims. After being released from prison he studied Agronomy, under the father's influence. However, although a distinguished student, he left Agronomy after three years and went to study law, which had always been his wish. He worked as a construction site director at the Perucica dam and was decorated for his outstanding contribution to a successful completion of the project. That is where he met Tito in 1958.

The largest part of the book (six chapters) deals with Izetbegovic's political activity after 1989. The most interesting details are related to vital political proposals and decisions: the attempt to reconstruct Yugoslavia, together with a Macedonian president Kiro Gligorov; decision to enter into a partnership with other two national parties rather than with civic parties; a so called historical accord between Serbs and Bosniacs and the failure of the Quitiliero's plan.

The attempt to reconstruct Yugoslavia – Izetbegovic and Gligorov tried to preserve Yugoslavia by turning it into a loose federation/confederation. Izetbegovic claims that their proposal was generally accepted by the presidents of all the republics. However, the stumbling block was the Army. Milosevic wanted a unified Army, while Tudjman insisted on separate armies. Since neither side wanted to relent the attempt failed and Croatia declared independence.

Decision to enter into a partnership with SDS and HDZ – Some journalists and politicians suggested that it had been better if SDA had entered into a partnership with civic political parties rather than SDS and HDZ. Izetbegovic argues that this would have alienated a majority of Serbs and Croats. War would not have been avoided. The only difference is that in that case the war of aggression would have been replaced with a civil war.

Historical Accord between Serbs and Bosniacs – Izetbegovic explains why he could not accept a so called Historical Accord with Serbs, proposed by the MBO leadership. According to him the accord would have made Bosniacs second-class citizens in a rump Yugoslavia, i.e. Greater Serbia. Unlike many, Izetbegovic explains why the Accord would have not prevented the war. Croats would have rebelled, supported by The Republic of Croatia, which would have taken an active political and military role. A war would have been waged between Serbs and Croats and Bosnia and Herzegovina would have been a battlefield. Bosniacs would have been caught in crossfire between Serbs and Croats.

Quitiliero's Plan – After the war many Bosniac politicians, journalists and scholars accused Izetbegovic for not accepting the Quitiliero's plan. The plan envisaged transformation of Bosnia and Herzegovina into a confederation of three republics. According to the plan Bosniacs were offered 44%, Serbs 39% and 17% of the territory of Bosnia and Herzegovina. It was announced that Radovan Karadzic had accepted the plan. In a book 'Bosniak', Adil Zulfikarpasic claimed that Izetbegovic had been happy with the plan. He told Adil:" We've got a territory bigger than Slovenia." Several sources suggested that Izetbegovic was ready to sign, but that he was persuaded by Warren Zimmerman, a former USA ambassador to Yugoslavia, to reject the plan. Allegedly, Zimmerman later confessed that this was a biggest political mistake of his life. However, Izetbegovic claims that actually Serbs refused to sign the plan. Since he did not provide more details this important moment of the Bosnia and Herzegovina history should be the subject of further research.

The book contains many philosophical thoughts and ideas. Most of them were elaborated in *Islam between East and West*:differences between culture and civilisation, religion, atheism and morality, the relationship between Islam and the West. Unlike other Muslim scholars Izetbegovic does not think that the West is rotten. He claims that only a minority of people in the West are degenerate and destructive. Most people in the West are hardworking and responsible. West is clean, organised and educated. Islamic countries should adopt many positive values from the West.

Regarding his identity Alija Izetbegovic considers himself first Muslim, than European and Slav. He claims that his heart is Islamic and mind European, owing to the fact that he received Western education. His Slav identity is expressed in his love for Russian literature, especially Dostoyevsky.

In one of the interviews a journalist asked Izetbegovic to assess Tito's personality. He claimed that Tito was a good person on the top of a bad system. A proof for this he finds in the fact that Tito loved life and that a bad person cannot love life. It is interesting statement from someone who was twice imprisoned by the Titoist regime.

The book represents an interesting read in every respect. It is warmly recommended to readers.

The Bosniak – Adil Zulfikarpasic in Dialogue with Milovan Djilas & Nadezda Gace, First published as Bosnjak Adil Zulfikarpasic by the Bosniak Institute, Zurich 1996. First published in the United Kingdom by C. Hurst & Co. (Publishers) Ltd. in 1998, pp 194

The book 'The Bosniak – Adil Zulfikarpasic in Dialogue with Milovan Djilas & Nadezda Gace ', contains a four day conversation between the Bosniak businessman, historian, politician and political writer Adil Zulfikarapasic, the Communist dissident Milovan Djilas and a journalist Nadezda Gace. The conversation took place in Budapest in 1994. It unravels the story about a remarkable individual, a strong-willed and colourful person, whose life has been rich, turbulent, eventful and above everything unconventional.

Born in 1921 in a famous aristocratic family of *Bosnian begs* Adil Zulfikarpasic received a traditional and patriarchal, yet for the criteria of that time and environment a liberal upbringing. Unlike most of the families in his class, who were devastated by the Agrarian Reform, his family retained a significant wealth. In spite of this he joined *The Communist Youth* at the age of 15 and *The Communist Party of Yugoslavia* at the age of 17. The years that followed were fulfilled by political activities and extensive reading of the writers such as Romand Rollan, Ernst Toll and Anatol Francais and philosophers Marx, Engels, Feuerbach, Kant and Hegel for the sake of understanding of the principles of Dialectic Materialism.

When the Second World War started he joined the Partisan Movement. His native town Foca was burnt down by the Chetniks, who killed 40 members of his extended family. In 1942 he was captured by the Ustasha, who sentenced him to death. A capital punishment was converted into 20 years of imprisonment. Adil Zulfikarpasic managed to escape from the prison in Sremska Mitrovica and rejoin the Partisans in Croatia.

At the end of the war Adil Zulfikarpasic had a high rank of the colonel of The Yugoslav People's Army. He was appointed a deputy minister of trade in the first Bosnia and Herzegovina government. At the age of only 25 all doors were opened for a brilliant political and military career. Then, listening to the voice of his conscience, Adil Zulfikarpasic made a radical decision, which will change his life path forever. Disillusioned with the Communism, its marvellous promises and much less impressive deliveries of the promises, he decided to leave all privileges and to emigrate to the West.

Apart from the usual hardships and uncertainty which life in emigration brings Zulfikarpasic's circumstance was aggravated by his political background. There were threats from Chetniks and Ustashas, who considered him an enemy and also attempts by the Yugoslav counterintelligence (KOS) to abduct him and bring him back to Yugoslavia. He spent some time in Italy and Austria before he finally settled in Switzerland. In Austria, he met his future wife, Tatjana Niksic, a daughter of the war time minister in the Ustasha government, Dr Ante Niksic. It is interesting to mention, that his future father-in-law gave his blessings to a marriage of his daughter to Adil under the condition that he converts to Catholicism.

In the beginning Zulfikarpasic worked as a journalist, later as a lawyer, before he decided to set up his own business. His life in Switzerland has revolved around three areas; export-import company, which proved to be very successful, political writing and practical political activity. In the early 1960's he founded a periodical 'Bosanski Pogledi '(Bosnian Views), on which almost all the European embassies in Belgrade as well as more than fifty universities and Slav institutes were subscribed. Later, Zulfikarpasic founded the Bosniak Institute in Zurich, which contains almost 40,000 books classified in several sections entitled *Bosnica, Serbica, Croatica and Yugoslavica*.

His practical political activity was a complement to his political writing. Both of them aimed at affirmation of the Bosniak national identity and attempt to find a satisfactory political agreement in Yugoslavia. He was a vice president of the *Liberal International* and a member of *Democratic Alternative*. The latter gathered democratic non-nationalistic politicians from all parts of Yugoslavia, whose aim was to democratise Yugoslavia, not by overthrowing the communist system, but by reforming it. This moderate, compromising political attitude was caused by almost prophetic fear which Zulfikarpasic expressed in the beginning of the 1960's that if Communism collapses in Eastern Europe catastrophe can again befall the Yugoslav nations.

During his life as an émigré Zulfikarpasic dreamt of returning to Bosnia. His dream came true in 1990. He immediately embarked on political activity, establishing SDA (the Moslem Party of Democratic Action) together with Alija Izetbegovic. He hoped that the party would be modern, democratic, liberal and secular. Instead, he encountered religious fanaticism, intolerance, primitivism and incompetence. In the other two nationalistic parties the situation was not better; aggressive, primitive nationalism threatened to throw the country into a chaos.

He left SDA, together with a group of intellectuals and established MBO (Moslem Bosniak Organisation). He and his followers were declared traitors by the SDA. In the general populist climate the principles of a civic society were not in high demand. MBO got only two seats in the Assembly, one of them being a member of the Bosnian Academy, Philosophy Professor Muhamed Filipovic.

Adil Zulfikarpasic was once more at the centre of the political stage when he offered *The Historical Agreement* to the Serbian politicians. The agreement was along the lines of a proposal outlined several decades ago by *Democratic Alternative*; the union of states with common market, common currency or separate currencies with a single convertible exchange rate, common army and common foreign policy. Although the agreement was supposed initially to include only Bosniaks and Serbs it opened the possibility to be extended to all the Yugoslav nations. Alija Izetbegovic backed the agreement in the beginning but later reneged on his promises for unknown reasons.

The agreement was ditched and Zulfikarpasic witnessed his darkest prophecy coming true.

The book contains an interesting chapter about life in a traditional patriarchal family, its customs and system of values. Adil Zulfikarpasic makes an interesting comparison between the Bosnian mountains on the one hand and the Austrian and Swiss mountains on the other hand and its impact on living conditions and peoples' mentality.

The book has many interesting, mainly unknown details. For example, *Aladza,* the famous mosque in Foca, which was raised to the ground by the Chetniks in the last war, derives its name from a Turkish word for multi-coloured. When Chetniks conquered Foca they changed its name to Srbinje, thinking that Foca was a Turkish word. In fact, the name Foca was derived from the Armenian-Greek word Hvoca, which means soaking hides in water. In ancient times Foca was a lively merchant town in which a bulk of economic activity consisted from trading in leather.

Adil Zulfikarpasic is an excellent connoisseur of History. Parts of the book are like fragmented lectures in medieval and modern history. But above all the book is a testimony of an extraordinary ability of the Balkan politicians to sacrifice hundreds of thousands of people for their vanity, political career and wealth.

While Nadezda Gace acts as an interviewer Milovan Djilas is an interlocutor. He also has a deep knowledge of history and literature and nice literary expressions which can be recognised even in a translated text. The book represents an enjoyable read and is warmly recommended.

Milutin Propadovich: "The Appalling Story of Euro-American Meddling in Yugoslavia", American-Yugoslav Association JADRAN, Milwaukee, Wisconsin, 2003

The titla of the book is borrowed from a report written by an American journalist Demaree Bess. The report was published in *The Saturday Evening Post, May 24, 1941* under the title *"Our Frontier on the Danube-The Appalling Story of our Meddling in the Balkans"*

The relevance of this statement 50 years after it was written confirms the validity of the old French adage *Plus ca change plus c'est la meme chose* – more things change more they stay the same. Three times in the XX century, in 1941, 1944-1945 and in 1991 United States and a several European countries caused a series of catastrophes affecting the nations of Yugoslavia.

The book observes Euro-American meddling from political and moral points of view. A direct inspiration for writing the book the author received from a statement of the former British Prime Minister Margaret Thatcher, who said: "First, this is mainly a moral question". The book is a direct response to widespread accusations of the Serbs as main culprits for the wars in the former Yugoslavia. Milutin Propadovich states that the primary purpose of the book is the defence of the Serbian nation. Pointing out the media biases, misinformation, misrepresentation and sometimes outright lies he states that the share of responsibility for the Yugoslav tragedy lies also on shoulders of Slovenes, Croats, Muslims and Albanians. However, the main sting of his criticism is directed towards the major culprits, the governments of the United States, Germany, Austria and Vatican.

The book consists of seven chapters. The first, "19141, 1944 and 1945", deals with events which happened more than half a century ago. Propadovich explains how Roosevelt and Churchill pushed Yugoslavia into the war. The American position could be understood by a succinct statement of Arthur Bliss Lane, the minister to Yugoslavia from 1937 to 1941:"...If it is in the interest of Hitler's Germany to keep peace in the Balkans, the corollary suggest itself... that it is in the interest of the Allies to disturb that peace." He quotes David Stafford and Cecil Parrott, history professors, to prove that SOE (Special Operations Executive) played an active part in the overthrow of the Prince Regent's government.

The author also mentioned the bombardment of the several Serbian cities and towns in September 1944, causing a death of thousands of civilians. The bombardment was ordered by Tito and did not have any military aims. The political aim of these barbaric acts was to break the moral of Serbian people, who offered a little support to the communists during the war. What followed a month later was Churchill's virtual handover of Yugoslavia to Stalin and Tito's communists.

The second chapter, "Destruction of Yugoslavia-Foreign Factors", analyses in detail the role of foreign factors in destruction of Yugoslavia. Propadovich insists that an early recognition of Slovenia and Croatia was illegal from the point of view of the International law. A state seeking international recognition must meet the following criteria:

1. The government must be in control of the territory and in possession of the machinery of the state;
2. The government must have the consent of the people without substantial resistance to its administration;
3. The government has indicated its willingness to comply with its obligation under treaties and international law.

None of these conditions was fulfilled in the case of Croatia and the first two were not met later in the case of Bosnia and Herzegovina. The main culprit in the case of an early recognition of Slovenia and

Croatia was the government of Germany, i.e. its foreign minister Hans Dietrich Genscher. The behaviour of the German government could be explained by the new strategy of expansionism or a new *Drang nach Osten* policy.

The government of the United States was, however, the main culprit for the war in Bosnia and Herzegovina. On two occasions American politicians prevented an agreement between the Bosnian communities. First time, when they put the pressure on Alija Izetbegovic to abandon a so called Historical Agreement between Serbs and Muslims, initiated by Adil Zulfikarpasic, the leader of the minor MBO party. Second time, when all the three leaders in Bosnia and Herzegovina signed the **Lisbon Agreement** on 23rd February 1992, according to which Bosnia and Herzegovina would have been transformed into a confederation of three ethnic cantons. All the three leaders agreed that such a decentralised Bosnian state would be internationally recognised and sovereign without a referendum. Warren Zimmerman, the last American ambassador in Yugoslavia, persuaded Izetbegovic to renege on his signature and to carry on with the referendum, which directly led to the war. Propadovich correctly concluded that Americans had not cared about Bosnian Muslims. Rather common financial interests of big corporations and some Islamic countries could explain the behaviour of the American government.

The third chapter, "Disinformation Machines" treats media bias and political propaganda. Propadovich emphasises three areas:

1. Exaggerating number of casualties
2. Inflated number of raped women
3. Mortar attacks on civilians in Sarajevo

As far as the latter is concerned Propadovich argues that there is a strong evidence that the Muslim forces carried out mortar attacks in order to accuse the Serbs and provoke a massive NATO military intervention.

The fourth chapter, "August 1995 – Dayton – Paris", points out a decisive American role in creating, what Propadovich calls, a Frankenstein monster, i.e. the Dayton Bosnia and Herzegovina. The author emphasises one of the goals the USA wanted to achieve with the war in Bosnia and Herzegovina, to assert its world leadership. Americans wanted to pass a message to its European allies; there would not be a peace agreement without them. Several European journalists and politicians are quoted to deny this statement. As a matter of fact nothing is further from the truth. Americans obstructed every previous attempt of the Europeans to end up military hostilities in Bosnia and Herzegovina.

The fifth chapter, "Destruction of Yugoslavia – Internal Factors", analyses domestic forces and their role in break-up of Yugoslavia. The most important part of this chapter deals with the role played in the destruction of Yugoslavia by the Memorandum of the Serbian Academy of Science and Arts and Milosevic. Propadovich tries to exonerate both claiming that even before their appearance some Slovene and Croat politicians, even communist ones, had clear plans for secession. He claims that the largest part of the Memorandum deals with economic, political and social crisis in Yugoslavia, and only the small part with the constitutional position of Serbia in the Yugoslav federation, persecution of Serbs in Kosovo, and the unsatisfactory position of Serbs in Croatia. He also claims that while Milosevic was a pragmatist interested only in preserving power, Tudjman was undoubtedly a nationalist with a clear plan for Croatia's secession from Yugoslavia.

The latter conclusion was as accurate as it is sharp-minded. However, it does not exonerate Milosevic for his share of responsibility in destruction of Yugoslavia. Before the war his reign passed through three stages. The first one was marked with an **Anti-bureaucracy revolution** slogan. It had a significant attraction, not only in Serbia, but also in Croatia and Bosnia and Herzegovina. However, it was short-lived. It was replaced by the second stage that fears, unrelated to national issues were raised. Rumours were spread that the **Romanian type** of communism might be introduced in Yugoslavia. In the third stage, Milosevic played a nationalist card. He would have never won the first elections in Serbia without the support of Serbs from Bosnia and Herzegovina and Croatia.

A frequent change in Milosevic's tactics made a fertile soil for various conspiracy theories which are not altogether groundless. Some considered him an American product, whose support he enjoyed as long as he played their game in destruction of Yugoslavia.

Analysing the content of the *Islamic Declaration*, Propadovich infers that Izetbegovic was in favour of a theocratic Islamic state in Bosnia. He links this with the strategy of the Iranian government, according to which Bosnian Muslims are the springboard for the expansion of Islam in Europe. Careful reading of the Islamic Declaration, however, would not miss the following sentence:"Pakistan is our great hope". At the time when the Islamic Declaration was written Pakistan was the only Islamic country with a multi-party system (the legacy of the British colonial rule). This indicates that Izetbegovic preferred undoubtedly Islamic country combined with the European-style parliamentary democracy rather than a theocratic Islamic state.

The sixth chapter, "Kosovo:President Clinton's Address to the Nation-Campaigns of Deception", treats events in Kosovo before, during and after the war. Propadovich emphasises abuse and misinterpretation of history. He also gives evidence to prove the support which the KLA received from the USA and Germany before the war. The culmination of unfair and biased attitude reached a climax at Rambouillet, where the Serbian delegation was blackmailed with an unacceptable ultimatum. This was succinctly expressed in words of a high-level U.S. official who reportedly told journalists at Rambouillet:" We intentionally set the bar too high for the Serbs to comply. They need some bombing, and that's what they are going to get". Propadovich uses a several quotations from the statements of politicians and military leaders to explain the U.S. position regarding Kosovo. Their common denominator is that ...*the so-called credibility of NATO, and the United States intention to retain its leadership within NATO was the main reason for the aggression against Serbia/Yugoslavia*".

The concluding chapter, "The Latest Appalling Story of Euro-American Meddling in Yugoslavia", investigates the situation in Bosnia and Herzegovina and Kosovo after the war. It explains a dismal political and economic environment, dysfunctional state in Bosnia and Herzegovina and ethnic cleansing in reverse in Kosovo.

The book is primarily written as a defence of the Serbian people. It is therefore one-sided. It omits misdeeds of Serbs. However, only several pages are allocated to misdeeds of other Yugoslav nations. Propadovich is convinced that Yugoslavia was the best solution for all their nations and that all of them are to a certain degree victims of games and manipulations of the great powers.

The book is extremely well researched. It does not contain a single factual mistake. Propadovich espouses an enviable knowledge of historical background as well as the knowledge of the current events. The book ends with 25 pages of notes from various books, magazines, journals, newspapers, interviews and reports. Most of resources are in English except for a small number which are in Serbo-Croat and German. The book represents in every respect an interesting read.

James Pettifer:"The Kosova Liberation Army – Underground War to Balkan Insurgency, 1948-2001", Hurst & Company 2012, London

The book consists of 12 chapters. 1The Origins of a Guerrilla Army, 2. The Underground War 1950-1990, 3. A New Force in the Balkans 1990-1995, 4. Preparation for the Battle:A Handgun Army?, 5. Autumn 1997:The War is Defined, 6. A Liberated Drenica and Milosevic's First Offensive, 7. Summer 1998:Golghota Avoided, 8. The Gathering Storm:Autumn 1998, 9. Racak to Rambouillet:January-March 1999, 10. Alliance with NATO and Demobilisation of the KLA,11. Preshevo and Macedonian Sequel and 12. Epilogue. It also contains sixteen illustrations and five appendixes.

The first two chapters are introductory. They provide background information prior to the birth of the KLA.

The first chapter is a bit of a misnomer, since only first two pages and several paragraphs later in the text are devoted to guerrilla war. The chapter mainly deals with military history, and to a lesser extent with economic history, geography and the socio-economic structure of the region.

The second chapter explains how Kosovar Albanians found themselves in a very difficult situation after the defeat of Drenica uprising, without anybody's help and at the mercy of the Yugoslav security forces. Plans of uprising in Kosovo with the aim of overthrowing the Titoist regime in Yugoslavia, concocted by Enver Hoxha and Mehmet Shehu, with collaboration with Russians, never materialised. In such a situation resistance was confined to futile spying activities of Zijadin Qira and the isolated political activity of Adem Demaci.

In 1968 there were massive demonstrations in Kosovo which were crushed by the Yugoslav security forces. However, they had an impact leading to a new Yugoslav constitution in 1974, which granted Kosovo autonomy. Student demonstrations in 1981, requesting Kosovo to be awarded a status of republic, were brutally crushed by the Yugoslav security forces. In the 1980s Tirana co-operated with Belgrade, returning some exiled Kosovar Albanian insurgents to Yugoslavia, where they faced long imprisonment. The attitude toward Kosovo changed in Albania after the death of Enver Hoxha. His successor Ramiz Alia, showed more enthusiasm, allowing the first military training of Kosovars in the Tirana Defence Academy. Alia saw the Irish Republican Army (IRA) as a possible model for a Kosovar insurgent army.

Chapters 3-11 follow political and military events in the late 1980s and 1990s. When it was clear that the pacifist policy of the LDK leader Ibrahim Rugova was not working, militants and radicals decided to start with preparations of military actions. A Swiss town Arrau, prosperous, with its liberal-socialist political tradition, became the centre of Albanian immigration and played a vital part in creation of the KLA.

In the beginning the KLA adopted Enverist organisational horizontal structure, with no military hierarchy and leaving a lot of space for the initiative of the rank-and-file. However, in the later stage of struggle, this organisational structure proved to be inadequate. In the beginning military strategy was a Maoist and Guevarist, and not the one recommended by a Russian Theorist Ana Starinov, namely using explosions behind the enemy lines. The latter was applied only in 1997, when a Serbian Mayors of Pec's car was blown into the air.

Although the KLA started its existence as a Marxist-Leninist terrorist organisation, there were always strong nationalist elements in the army. Professor Pettifer claims that the KLA quickly ditched its ideological gown and that also distanced itself from any potential Islamic influence.

In the beginning KLA activists were confined to attacks on Serbian refugees from Croatia and police stations. The insurgents had a particularly strong grudge against police because of its notorious cruelty.

Belgrade tried to portray the KLA as a drug-financial criminal organisation, with no real support amongst Kosovar Albanian population. This image of the KLA prevailed for many years. Professor Pettifer mentions Saint Egidio initiative, created by several Vatican officials. The purpose of the initiative was to organise negotiations between more moderate Albanian politicians and Milosevic with the view of restoring 1974 style autonomy for Kosovo within the rump Yugoslav federation. Most Vatican dignitaries did not want the creation of a majority Muslim Kosovo independent state, fearing for the rights of the 12% of Kosovar Albanians who are Catholic.

The conflict intensified in 1997. The uprising in Albania gave a boost to the KLA since weapons started flowing over the border to Kosovo. As a result the KLA liberated Drenica and controlled the area east of the Mitrovica-Prishtina road. In such a situation Milosevic wanted to involve the army, since police forces could not deal with insurgents. The chief of staff, General Momcilo Perisic, was against army involvement, claiming that the conflict in Kosovo is an internal affair and that the army should be involved only to protect Yugoslav borders. Because of his stance he was replaced in 1998 by a militant and radical general Nebojsa Pavkovic. The army mainly shelled villages, causing hundreds of thousands of refugees to be internally displaced within Kosovo. Still, the KLA members, who served the Yugoslav People's Army, easily noticed a sharp decline in the strength of the VJ. A lack of spare parts, inadequate training, irregular payments and out-dated equipment made the VJ a pale shadow of once upon a time the fourth strongest army in Europe.

The KLA still had a reputation of a terrorist organisation, detached from a majority of Kosovo Albanians. This image was particularly held by some British officials, who had strong Yugoslav leanings. In addition, some British officials were afraid of too much Communist influence in the KLA.

Things changed in 1998, when Madeleine Albright and Richard Holbrooke insisted that any political deal between the Serbs and Albanians must include the KLA. Also, Paddy Ashdown suggested air strikes against Serbia.

After the Racak Massacre more pressure was put on Milosevic to start western sponsored negotiations with the Albanian side. Negotiations were held in Rambouillet, ending in NATO strikes against Serbia, followed by the *Operation Horse-shoe*, undertaken by the Yugoslav Army, Serbian police forces and paramilitaries, whose aim was to expel as many Albanians as possible from Kosovo. After 78 days, the war ended with the Serbian forces handing over Kosovo0 to NATO. This was followed by disarmament of the KLA and Kosovo independence in 2008.

The epilogue summarises the events and briefly deals with several issues, such as the events in Presevo valley in 2000 and in FYROM in 2001. It expresses concern that a limited and controlled independence of Kosovo can make the young state fragile and that Serbia can raise a border issue sometime in the future. Also, if Kosovo proves to be economically unviable Serbia might try to convince Kosovar Albanians that they would be better off as a part of their country. In other words, there are fears that the independence might be reversible.

The book follows political and military developments throughout history, with the emphasis on a period after the WWII. The political analysis is biased. It is anti-Serbian and also anti-Yugoslav. It failed to recognise the following:

First, the conflict in Kosovo is a clash between a historical right, which belongs to the Serbs, and an ethnic right, which belongs to the Albanians. It resembles a conflict in Palestine between the historical right, which belongs to the Jews and the ethnic right, which belongs to the Palestinian Arabs. In 1947 the United Nations endorsed a partition of Palestine and formation of the two states. Jews accepted and Palestinian Arabs refused. More moderate Serbs were ready to offer Albanians a broad autonomy, or partition, in which they would retain 20-25% of Kosovo, mainly in the North and at the fringes in the western part of the province. Albanians refused, and the International community supported them. Therefore, different standards were applied in Palestine and Kosovo.

Second, Albanians had a rough deal after the two wars because of the weakness of their mother country. The first, royalist Albania was a puppet of Yugoslavia before 1930 and afterwards a puppet of Italy, without whose help would have been an unviable state. The second, communist Albania was also a poor, isolated country with bad international reputation. In such a situation not many people noticed that the Albanian national question was the second most difficult national problem in Europe (after the Basques' national problem).

Things improved significantly after the 1974 Yugoslav constitution granted Kosovo autonomy short of a status of republic. Kosovo received $1.4m. in aid every day from The Fund for development of Underdeveloped Republics and Autonomous Provinces. Prishtina university was opened, providing education in Albanian language to tens of thousands young Albanians, mainly in social and humanistic sciences. These developments created a social and intellectual basis for a coherent national consciousness; a different quality from sporadic and futile killings of Serb colonists and a few gendarmes before the WWII, when Kosovo had two PhD holders and less than 1% adults with a university degree.

Third, Yugoslavia reacted differently in 1981 and in 1987. In 1981 the whole of Yugoslavia was united in condemnation of Albanian demonstrators who demanded Kosovo to be granted a status of republic. The most brutal were members of Slovene police forces, who threw Albanian students from the fourth floor onto the street. Slovenes were particularly furious since they paid most to Kosovo, being the most developed republic in Yugoslavia. It could be hardly said, however, that the members of the special units from Slovenia were ill-educated.

The response of the rest of Yugoslavia was quite different in 1987. Serbs remained isolated, and most of Yugoslavia supported the Albanians when Milosevic decided to abolish Kosovo's autonomy.

Finally, Professor Pettifer mentioned that in-spite of the Belgrade's propaganda there were no contacts between the KLA and Al-Qaeda. Using a book "Reconsidering Kosovo", I mentioned the meeting between the KLA leaders and Osama bin Laden in Tirana in 1995 in my article:"Independent Kosovo in the Context of the Declining American Hegemony". This is hardly a secret. Several sources of information about the meeting are available on the internet. This, however, does not say anything about the nature of the KLA. Slovenes also had contacts with Al-Qaeda before Slovenia declared its independence. Ironically, this also confirms Professor Pettifer's conclusion that Serbian political marketing was counterproductive. Serbs bet on the wrong horse, since devout Muslims and Islamic fundamentalists are rarities in Kosovo.

But, then, this is a book about the KLA. As such it is well researched, detailed, exhaustive and brilliantly written. The analysis of the KLA is multifaceted:historical, political, cultural, socioeconomic, ideological, military and even psychoanalytical. Professor Pettifer exudes with more than impressive erudition.

The bibliography and resources are equally impressive, and include works in six languages:English, Albanian, German, French, Italian and Serbian.

I warmly recommend this book to all interested in the region.

Tonny Brems KInudsen and Carsten Bagge Lausten:"Kosovo between War and Peace – Nationalism, Peace-building and International Trusteeship", published by Routledge, OXON, 2006

The book 'Kosovo between War and Peace – Nationalism, Peace-building and International Trusteeship' is the collection of articles dealing with theoretical and empirical aspects of post-war issues related to Kosovo. As the title indicates the book consists of three areas of research. Two chapters deal with the issues of nationalism, myths and revenge. Four chapters are devoted to the key aspects of the on-going reconstruction; the performance of UNMIK, local governance and democracy, educational system and crime and capitalism. Three chapters research the role of international trusteeship and its impact on national self-determination, state sovereignty and the future status of Kosovo.

Lene Kuhle and Carsten Bagge Laustsen in their article 'The Kosovo myth – Nationalism and revenge seek the explanation for the Kosovo conflict in Serb and Albanian myth. The Serb myth revolves around the battle of Kosovo Field in 1389 between the Serb-led coalition of Christian countries and the Ottoman Empire. According to the myth a falcon representing Saint Elijah and a swallow representing Virgin Mary came to Serbian prince Lazar at the battlefield and offered him a choice. If he attacks the Ottomans immediately he will win. If not, he can choose the Kingdom of

Heaven and eternal glory, lose the battle and build a church in Kosovo and call his men to communion. Lazar chose the Kingdom of Heaven. The Serbs lost the battle, their empire crumbled and they were enslaved by the Turks for more than four centuries.

The Serb myth is shaped to the Christian model. Prince Lazar represents Christ, Vuk Brankovic Iuda Iskariot, Kosovo maiden Mary Magdalene and Jugovic's mother Virgin Mary. By choosing the Heavenly Kingdom Serbs became elected people. Kosovo is therefore, for Serbs not only the cradle of their medieval state but also a hub of their national identity. For Serbs, Kosovo is what Jerusalem is for Jews.

Albanians tried to build their myth along similar lines. The Albanian national poet Naim Frasheri who lived in the XIX century used the battle of Kerbala in 680 to introduce Shiite symbols in developing the Albanian myth. Prophet Muhammed's grandson was killed in the battle. He was offered a choice between allegiance to caliph Yazid, which would make him a traitor, or resistance to him which would lead to his certain death. He chose to resist and became a martyr. However, being a Shiite in its origin, the myth failed to unite different factions of Albanian Moslems, which consisted of Sunnis, Shiites and the members of the Sufi order. The Albanian myth was built on the presumption that they originate from the ancient Illyrians, who lived in the area long before the Slavs came. Therefore, they claim the right of the first occupiers. The authors of the article see the glimpse of hope in midst of conflicting myths in the fact that after the war contacts between the two religious communities, Albanian and Serb, have been more intensive than between their secular counterparts.

Arne Johan Vetlesen in his article 'The logic of genocide and the prospects of reconciliation' introduces a new treatment of genocide. In the 1948 Genocide Convention genocide is defined as:".... *acts committed with intent to destroy, in whole or in part, a national, ethnical, racial or religious group as such*'. Vetlesen claims that intent weighs heavier than extent. Therefore, genocide does not need to imply a physical destruction. A group could physically exist, or escape total extermination, but in a process is left so marginalised and traumatised or so irrelevant to society that became effectively dysfunctional.

The process of reconciliation requires an active participation of a third party. Only if a third party is involved the versions of the both parties could be heard and a proper judgement could be made. Reconciliation assumes rejection of the concept of *Kolektiv Schuld* and identifying individuals responsible for crimes and atrocities instead. The process of reconciliation might involve acquittal for those who admit crimes and therefore the sacrifice of justice for the sake of lasting peace.

In his article 'Local Governance in Kosovo-a link to Democratic Development'? Mark Baskin argues that efficient, accountable and transparent local governance is vital in expressing genuine interests of citizens. He states that local governance requires sufficient security to enable officials and citizens to pursue their livelihoods in physical safety. Democratic local governance also relies upon freedom of movement, freedom of expression, assembly and participation. This depends on effectiveness of the police and judiciary system. Baskin praises efforts made by Kosovo Police Service to support democratic local governance. The service has been successful in providing high quality training and maintaining ethnic and gender balance in recruitment, with minorities willing to speak a non-native language when the situation requires. However, a development of democratic local governance is faced with serious impediments caused by a low level of economic development, high unemployment, a lack of fiscal resources, reluctance of central authorities to delegate more power to municipal level, corruption and continuing politicisation of public life and growing apathy among ordinary citizens.

In the article "Foundations and Fractures of Kosovo's Educational System – Towards Conflict or Peace?" Wayne Nelles argues that in Kosovo education has been a core issue around which many socioeconomic, political and ethnic problems are revolved. She states that Department of Education and Science under UNMIK regulations stressed that that one of its functions was: '*the promotion of a single unified, non-discriminatory and inclusive education system so that each person's right to education is respected and quality learning opportunities are available to all, irrespective of their ethnic or social origin, race or gender, disability, religion, or political opinion*'. However, in spite of these proclamations ethnic minorities remain in disadvantageous position and parallel education systems are developed along ethnic lines.

In the article 'Crime and capitalism in Kosovo's transformation' Michael Pugh explains how the principles of neo-liberalism were imposed on Kosovo's economy after the war. Although those principles were not harshly implemented like elsewhere, since considerable attention was paid to social policies, it still failed to produce desirable results. Economic growth is sluggish and unemployment is highest in Europe. This state of affairs led to a growth of a shadow economy which generates more than 50% of GDP. A shadow economy contributes to an increase in production, consumption, income and the standard of living, but at the same time prevents the development of legal market economy. In order to change this state of affairs Michael Pugh suggests neo-liberal approach to economic development to be replaced by the principles of Keynesian economy, with the stronger link to local economies.

In his article '**Administering membership of international society**-The role and function of UNMIK' Rasmus Abildgaard Kristensen analyses positive versus negative sovereignty and territorial versus ethnic self-determination. He stated that positive sovereignty in the interwar period was replaced by negative sovereignty after the Second World War. However, after the Cold War positive sovereignty has been again imposed by the international community. He blames inconsistency of the international arrangements rather than UNMIK for the failure to find the solution for Kosovo conundrum. The principle *uti possidetis iuris* opens the legal possibility for independence of Kosovo. However, this clashes with positive sovereignty and ethnic self-determination.

In his article '**From UNMIK to self-determination?** – The puzzle of Kosovo's future status' Tonny Brems Knudsen analyses pluralistic and solidarist (Grotian) conception of international society. In the view of these two concepts he sees five potential solutions for Kosovo:1) The indefinite continuation of Kosovo as an international protectorate, 2) partition of the province, 3) autonomy within Serbia, 4) conditional independence and 5) full independence. Tonny Brems Knudsen favours conditional independence with indefinite limited trusteeship in which Serbia would have a significant input.

In the article '**Liberal Trusteeship**-The convergence of interest and ideology in international administration' Christopher P. Freeman states that liberal trusteeship operates according to three component ambitions:peace maintenance, economic restructuring/discipline and socialisation. In the liberal ideology all three are seen as inseparable, and human rights makes the project morally admissible and often desirable to liberal policies. However, there are serious impediments in implementation of these principles. Increased porosity of borders and inability of neo-liberal policy to tackle social problems increases the significance of the shadow economy and the network of informal institutions, undermining a state sovereignty.

The articles in the book cover all the topics relevant to the Kosovo problem. The authors have conducted research thoroughly and meticulously. Some contain more than 90 references, which would be an impressive bibliography even for a book. However, articles which deal with the final status of the province lack creativity and originality. Most authors are in favour of conditional independence, although they are aware that this solution might set a dangerous precedence and cause a domino effect throughout Europe. A broad autonomy of Kosovo combined with increasing Balkan integration, which would include Albania, was not considered. Such a solution would be facilitated in the new world environment in which the Westfalian system is replaced by more transparent borders between states and less rigid concept of state sovereignty. In spite of this the book is excellent and is warmly recommended to readers.

Michael Waller, Kyril Drezov and Bullent Gokay (editors):"Kosovo – The politics of delusion" Frank Cass Publishers, London 2001

The book 'Kosovo-The Politics of Delusion', is a collection of essays emerged as a result of six seminars which took place in Keele and Cambridge between 26 October 1998 and 15 December 1999. It contains objective and neutral assessment of the situation in the province as well as highly emotionally charged opinions about the rights and wrongs of NATO intervention.

The book examines both the escalation of the Kosovo conflict to a full-scale war and the aftermath of the war. It consists of two parts. The first part deals with the background and history of the conflict. The second part gives different opinions on NATO military attack on FRY and consequent occupation of Kosovo. The book ends with a separate section containing documents related to Kosovo and a chronology of events.

The first part deals with the issues of conflicting myths, Albanian school system in Kosovo, Kosovo Liberation Army, the role of Albanian governments in Kosovo problem, Kosovo refugees in Albania during the war, international law in Kosovo and collateral damage. Aleksandar Pavkovic explains the conflict in Kosovo as a result of conflicting myths. The Serbian myth sees Kosovo as a cradle of the medieval Serbian state, the sacred land and the focal point of the Serbian national identity. For Serbs Kosovo is what is Jerusalem for the Jews. Albanians consider themselves the descendants of the ancient Illyrians, who lived in Kosovo long before Slavs settled in the Balkans.

They therefore claim the right to Kosovo as the first occupiers, and consequently all other nations, including Serbs can live in Kosovo only as their guests. After the WW2 communists tried to create the third multiethnic myth, by denying the previous two myths, according to which no ethnic group has an exclusive right on Kosovo, but all of them should share the land peacefully. However, the communists failed to eradicate the two national myths inspite the repression undertaken for almost a half of the century. In conclusion Pavkovic points out that one could imagine another liberation of all inhabitants of Kosovo by securing political and civil liberties for all its citizens. However, to achieve this kind of liberation the peoples in Kosovo would need to liberate themselves from the very myths of national liberation, which have for so long justified violence and atrocities to other ethnic groups.

Denisa Kostovicova emphasizes a close historical link between politics and education in Kosovo. Political control by one ethnic group in the province has usually led to a denial of education to the other. She explains that the constitution in 1974, which gave Kosovo a quasi republic status in Yugoslavia, has resulted in the spread of education among Albanians at various levels of educational process. Although the knowledge of national history and literature was strictly consigned to those personalities who promoted a common life in the Yugoslav socialist state it nevertheless enabled Albanians to discover their national identity both in opposition to Serbs as well as in terms of fraternity with Albanians in Albania. This process was put in reverse after the Serbian constitution virtually abolished the province's autonomy in 1989. Albanians organized a parallel state with a parallel education system, which surprisingly was tolerated by the Serbian authorities. However, a widespread joblessness among Kosovo Albanians, caused by a mass dismissal of Albanians from state-owned enterprises, shrank a tax base of financing education, whose quality eroded over the period of 1990's.

Tim Judah and James Pettifer explore the origins and the rise of the KLA (Kosovo Liberation Army). Created in 1990's as a Marxist-Leninist terrorist organization the KLA numbered only a few hundred members in 1997. There were several factors which contributed to a rise of KLA from a negligible organization to a significant force one needed to reckoned with in the Balkan matters. First, geo-politics, in a sense that spreading the Kosovo conflict to the neighboring countries was unacceptable to the international community. Second, that Albanian population in Kosovo was disillusioned with a pacifist approach of Ibrahim Rugova and especially disappointing outcome of the Dayton Accord, which did not address the Kosovo problem at all. Third, the pyramid scheme collapse in Albania and subsequent lawlessness enabled the KLA to acquire substantial stocks of weaponry and ammunition. As a result the KLA managed to provoke the Federal army militarily and to achieve a few temporary victories. At Rambouillet negotiation talks it was the KLA political leader Hashim Taci, not Ibrahim Rugova, who was leading the Kosovo Albanian delegation.

Miranda Vickers describes how attitudes of various Albanian governments in Tirana fluctuated in regards to the Kosovo problem. The first democratically elected government of Salih Berisha had to change its tune and abandoned the claim for independent Kosovo under the pressure from Western governments. The socialist governments of Fattos Nano and Pandel Majko advanced the view that Kosovo should be a third Yugoslav republic alongside Serbia and Montenegro. At the same time the Albanian government turned a blind eye to arming of the KLA, whose overt aim was an independent Kosovo.

Alba Bozo talks about the reception of Kosovo refugees in Albania. Out of 478,000 refugees 300,000 were hosted by Albanian local families. This fact strengthened the feeling of national identity and solidarity among Albanians and restored Albania's pride and changed the image of the country as a land of chaos and anarchy.

Patrick Thornberry discusses the legal issues concerning NATO military intervention in Kosovo. He refuses the main argument in favour of the intervention, the humanitarian one. There was no doctrine of humanitarian intervention recognized in international law. Besides, the unilateral action, unauthorized by the United Nations is illegal from the point of view of the international law. Apart from that he discards the case for humanitarian intervention because there was no genuine humanitarian purpose and high-altitude bombing, use of anti-personnel weapons further disqualified the mission as humanitarian.

Kyril Drezov analyses the collateral damage which the war in Kosovo inflicted on Macedonia. He claims that since the early 1990's Macedonia's stability was based on three fundamentals; state monopoly in the means of violence, Slav domination of the state and Western support of the state. Even before NATO's involvement in the Kosovo conflict, these fundamentals of Macedonia's stability were negatively affected by the collapse of the central government in Albanian 1997, which made weapons available to Kosovo and Macedonian Albanians, and the termination of UNPREDEP in February 1999, following a Chinese veto after Skopje's recognition of Taiwan. The influx of refugees from Kosovo into Macedonia threatened to alter a fragile multiethnic balance between Macedonians and Albanians. Macedonians feared that a repeated Kosovo scenario in Macedonia and another NATO's involvement in drawing a line between the two conflicting sides would be perceived locally as victory for the Albanians, and would mark the end of Macedonia as a nation-state.

The second part of the book presents different opinions on the NATO military intervention in Kosovo. Opposing views of this issue reflect a tension between principles of international law, which emphasize state sovereignty and those which value human rights. Those who supported the intervention include Christopher Brewin, Alex Danchev and Matthew Wyman. Kyril Drezov, Bulent Gokay, Andrew Fear, John Sloboda, Sofia Damm and Andrew Dobson condemned NATO's military involvement in Kosovo. Michael Waller and Martin Dent offered more balanced views, considering objectively arguments for and against the NATO's attack on FRY.

The case against NATO's military intervention was built on the following premises:1) The NATO's attack on FRY was illegal from the point of view of international law. 2) There was no case for humanitarian intervention. Humanitarian intervention was a smoke screen, whose aim was to conceal the real motives; NATO's credibility and USA wider strategic goals. 3) USA applies double standards and turns a blind eye on the violation of human rights in friendly countries, i.e. persecution of Kurds by the Turkish government. 4) So called humanitarian intervention caused a humanitarian disaster since unprotected Albanian civilians were left at the mercy of the Serbian forces. 5) The conduct of a high-altitude bombing did not comply with the main principles in waging a war, namely discrimination, necessity and proportionality. As a result collateral damage was enormous. 6) After the war ethnic cleansing in reverse occurred in Kosovo with Serbs and Roma being expelled by the KLA. 7) The war strengthen Milosevic's position in power. 8) The military intervention did not contribute to the solution of the Kosovo problem.

The case for the intervention was based on the following arguments:1) A pacifist policy of Ibrahim Rugova did not produce any results. 2) Even before the war humanitarian situation in Kosovo was difficult (Massacres in Drenica and Racak) with hundreds of thousands of refugees and internally displaced persons. 3) Milosevic is a dictator who understands only one language, the language of force. 4) The intervention opened up the possibility of the solution of the Kosovo problem etc.

Most of the articles in the second part of the book were written either during or immediately after the war. Some/ many predictions of the authors have not come through. In general, though, the book covers all the relevant aspects of the Kosovo war and the Kosovo problem. It is written by highly competent experts and it represents a very interesting read.

Alaistair Finlan:"The Collapse of Yugoslavia 1991-1999" Osprey Publishing, Oxford, England, 2004

The book 'The Collapse of Yugoslavia 1991-1999' is a synopsis of events which preceded and followed the break-up of Yugoslavia. The author states that the collapse of Yugoslavia represents one of the greatest and at the same time one of the least understood tragedies in recent times. The war in the former Yugoslavia is surrounded by myths. One of them is that for centuries there has been a tension between various ethnic groups which occasionally erupted into violent conflicts. Alastair Finlan tackles this simplistic approach to a break-up of Yugoslavia. He considers the events in former Yugoslavia unique in historical perspective. While conflicts usually involve two sides the war in former Yugoslavia engaged multiple protagonists. Finlan identifies thirteen active and passive players in the conflict. They are **Bosnian Croats, Bosniacs, Bosnian Serbs, Croatians, Croatian Serbs, Kosovars, Macedonians, Montenegrins, Serbians, Slovenians, Vojvodinas, the NATO and the UN.** To these participants one could add NGO and unofficial groups comprising bandits, criminals, mercenaries and smugglers. A huge number of participants with different interests added to the complexity of the situation and made it extremely hard for the international community to understand the real nature of the conflict and to react appropriately.

Finlan points out that right from the start the war in the former Yugoslavia was an uneven contest. He describes in detail with astonishing competence a military superiority of Serbian forces in terms of military equipment. In such a situation the arms embargo, imposed by the UN on all the participants in the conflict helped to maintain a status quo, forcing other players to rely on smuggled weapons. Conflicting interests among the major EU countries were an impediment to creation of a unified EU approach to the war.

Finlan critisizes the role of the UN generally secretary Boutros-Boutros Gali and his special representative Yasushi Akashi for their 'soft approach' to the conflict. The same criticism is directed to the British government of John Major, which was resolutely against any decisive joint military action. At the same time Finlan points out that the British government was most generous in delivering humanitarian aid; food and medicines as well as troops on the ground. Finlan describes a few heroic actions conducted by the British troops in their humanitarian mission. A whole chapter is dedicated to Lieutenant-colonel Bob Stewart, who saved 150 Bosniacs from death during the conflict between ABiH and HVO in Central Bosnia in 1993.

Indecisiveness of the British government transpires to be a biased approach in favour of the Bosnian Serbs. Finlan reveals a detail which corroborates his assessment of the attitude of the British government to the conflict. After retiring from the post of the foreign minister Douglas Herd travelled to Belgrade in 1996 to try to obtain a contract with Milosevic's government to offer advice on privatization.

During the war there was an impression that international military commanders on the ground had their hands tied up by a very complicated procedure. Finlan reveals that they actually had a great deal of autonomy in decision making. He criticizes the French general Janvier and the British general Sir Michael Rose for not requesting NATO air strikes. According to Finlan General Sir Michael Rose could have ended up the war a year and a half earlier if he had requested a decisive NATO action in April 1994 during the Serb offensive on Gorazde.

Unlike his predecessors General Sir Rupert Smith was more decisive and showed much more initiative. At the end of August 1995 he circumvented the UN and the countries which contributed troops to UNPROFOR and talked directly with the head of NATO's Southern Command who eventually initiated the air strikes, precipitating the end of the war. The direct beneficiaries of this action were the victims of the Serbian aggression, especially the Bosniacs, who managed to involve the only remaining superpower in the conflict. Finlan assesses The Dayton Agreement as a good temporary solution. However, he thinks that the Agreement will be changed some time in the future when the situation permits. New negotiations, in his view, will take place between the three sides and without interference of the international community.

The last chapter of the book deals with the war in Kosovo in 1999. Finlan just briefly stated that the Albanians accepted and the Serbs refused the Rambouillet Agreement. However, he did not mention the reasons for the Serbian refusal i.e. unrestricted access to the NATO troops throughout the whole of territory of The Federal Republic of Yugoslavia and a referendum on the independence of Kosovo in three years time.

The book contains many black and white and colour pictures. It also provides several maps:The Map of the Former Yugoslavia, The Map of Balkan War Zone 1992-1994, The Map of Vance-Owen Peace Plan, The Map of Safe Areas in Bosnia and Herzegovina and The Dayton Agreement Map. The book is a concise, accurate and useful reminder of the events in the former Yugoslavia from 1991 to 1999.

Michael Mandel:"How America Gets Away With MURDER-Illegal Wars, Collateral Damage and Crimes against Humanity", Pluto Press, London 2004

The book 'How America Gets Away With MURDER' deals with the three wars which USA waged at the end of the XX century and at the beginning of the XXI century, namely the wars in the Federal Republic of Yugoslavia, Afghanistan and Iraq. The central thesis of the book is that all the three wars were illegal from the point of view of the international law and that therefore they represent crimes against humanity.

The first part of the book entitled **Illegal Wars/Collateral Damage** has three chapters. They deal with the legal analysis of the three wars in a reverse chronological order. The war in Iraq was analysed first as the most brilliant example of an aggressive and illegal war. Professor Mandel explains that from the point of view of the international law there are only three cases which make war legal; a war waged for self-defence, a war authorised by the Security Council of the United Nations and a war waged as humanitarian intervention. Although USA tried to use all the three criteria to justify the war in Iraq none of them can pass a legal test. A self-defence criterion is not valid since USA was not attacked by Iraq and peaceful means in finding the weapons of mass destruction were not exhausted. Using this criterion many countries in the world would have a good reason to attack USA, which has the largest stock of the weapons of mass destruction. Above all, Iraq apparently did not have the weapons of mass destruction otherwise it would have used it during the war.

USA did not even try to seek the authorisation of the Security Council of the United Nations knowing that unlike in 1991 the resolution sanctioning the war would not pass since three permanent members, Russia, China and France would use the veto.

According to international law the right for humanitarian intervention can be exercised only as a collective right, authorised by the Security Council of the United Nations. This clause was introduced in The Charter of the United Nations after the WW2 in order to avoid the unilateral humanitarian interventions such as those undertaken by the Nazi Germany, allegedly to protect the human rights of endangered German minorities in the neighbouring countries. Since the authorisation for humanitarian intervention in Iraq was not given by the Security Council of the United Nations, USA-led war against Iraq does not differ from the legal point of view from the Nazi aggression on Czechoslovakia and Poland. In both cases although the wars were legal from the point of view of the German and American law, they were illegal from the point of view of the international law. Also, the invasion of Iraq led to a significant deterioration in human rights in that country compared to the period of Saddam's reign. Professor Mandel discloses American hypocrisy in using humanitarian intervention as an excuse for the invasion. He recalls that Saddam's brutality was condoned and tacitly supported by the USA during the 1980's when he was an American ally. In conclusion, professor Mandel states that "the world was convinced that this was not the war fought because of some new realities of terrorism, weapons of mass destruction, much less for 'freedom', but rather for the old familiar reasons of empire:private wealth and public strategic power."

The second chapter analyses the war in Afghanistan. The war was waged in November 2003, two months after the terrorist attack on The World Trade Centre in New York. This gave the claim of 'self-defence' a superficial plausibility that the war against Iraq lacked. However, Article 33 of the Charter of the United Nations requires that the parties to any dispute first seek a peaceful solution through negotiations, enquires, mediations etc. before resorting to violent means. Taliban supreme leader Mullah Omar was willing to co-operate with the USA. He asked the Americans to provide the evidence of bin Laden's involvement in 11/09 attack before putting him on trial. But even if the Americans had the proof and if bin Laden did not leave Afghanistan, they did not have the right to invade Afghanistan. Professor Mandel draws a parallel with the abduction of Adolf Eichmann from Argentina, conducted by the Mossad in 1961. Although the Israelis did not harm anyone during the operation they were unanimously condemned by the Security Council.

USA also used humanitarian-intervention as an excuse for the invasion of Afghanistan. Although the whole world accepted that the Taliban authorities widely abused human rights, especially the rights of women, the evidence shows that the situation has deteriorated after the war. American allies, the Northern Alliance, upon usurping power proclaimed, among other things, the compulsory veiling of all women. In terms of widespread raping of girls and women Taliban was no match to the soldiers of the Northern Alliance.

The third chapter is devoted to the war in Kosovo. Unlike the wars in Iraq and Afghanistan, the only justification for the war in Kosovo was humanitarian intervention. Professor Mandel proves that USA created humanitarian disaster by deliberate obstruction of the political process, whose aim was to find the political solution for the Kosovo problem. He explains in detail negotiations which took place in Rambouillet in France. NATO set 'non-negotiable principles', which included an immediate end to hostilities, broad autonomy for Kosovo with an executive, legislative and judicial power, elections within nine months, respect of the rights of all persons and ethnic groups and the territorial integrity of the Federal Republic of Yugoslavia. Serbs immediately accepted these principles, but Albanians complained that they did not go far enough regarding the independence of Kosovo. They also requested the presence of the NATO forces. Under the pressure from the Albanian side the agreement was re-drafted to give them two vital concessions; unrestricted and free access of NATO forces to all facilities throughout the Federal Republic of Yugoslavia and a referendum in three years on independence of Kosovo. Serbs were presented with the ultimatum which no independent country in the world could have accepted. When the bombing campaign started the Serbian security forces were left free on the ground to undertake the wholesale ethnic cleansing. The war resulted in thousands of casualties on the both sides, more than a million people expelled and displaced and huge destruction of property. Even after hostilities ended the situation regarding human rights did not significantly improved, and remains much worse than before the war. KLA undertook ethnic cleansing in reverse, expelling non-Albanians, mainly Serbs and Roma/Gypsies. The murder rate is highest in the world, 20 times higher than in the Western Europe. Professor Mandel correctly states that Americans did not care about the rights of Albanians. The war in Kosovo was waged for the USA strategic interests outside of the Balkans.

All the three wars were accompanied by so-called collateral damage. Collateral damage refers to casualties among non-combatants, i.e. civilians, and destruction of property. The USA and its allies knew that collateral damage is inevitable, in-spite of highly sophisticated military technology. They claim that the fundamental difference between them and terrorists is that collateral damage caused by a bombing campaign is not intentional. Professor Mandel proves that in legal theory there is no difference between intentional and knowing killing. He uses a legal concept of 'transferred intent' to prove that the bombing campaign undertaken by NATO represents the highest level of terrorism, collective or so-called state terrorism.

The second part of the book entitled **Crimes against Humanity** consists of four chapters; The War Crimes Tribunals, The Trial of Milosevic, America Gets Away with Murder and Rounding up The Usual Suspects While America gets Away With Murder. In the fourth chapter Professor Mandel explains in detail that ICTY (International Criminal Tribunal for Yugoslavia) was established even before the war in Kosovo and that was used throughout as a political tool of the USA. He also states the role of the media, who very often used the Holocaust metaphor to strengthen the case against the Serbs. Also, he mentioned that in an official letter of protest Federal Republic of Yugoslavia government listed many armed conflicts where war crimes were committed and whose perpetrators have not been punished or prosecuted. The most recent examples include general Augusto

Pinochet and Ariel Sharon. In other words ICTY was an exercise in double standards.

In the fifth chapter Professor Mandel explains that Milosevic's extradition to the Hague was unconstitutional because the Yugoslav constitution forbade the extradition of nationals preferring to try them in domestic courts, following an ancient maxim **aut dedere aut iudiciare**. President Kostunica had to withdraw the legislation and to replace it with government decree – a very dubious tactic from the constitutional point of view. When the trial started Milosevic was accused of genocide, although the facts about the number of victims cannot fit into its definition. Also, during the trial Milosevic was not allowed to proceed with the questioning of witnesses whenever they were cornered by his arguments.

In the sixth chapter Professor Mandel builds the case against NATO. He mentioned many complaints coming from individuals and groups around the world demanding prosecution of NATO leaders. The case against NATO was based on two distinct kinds of crime within the jurisdiction of the Tribunal:'crimes against humanity' and 'crimes against the laws and customs of war.' Professor Mandel added the third one;'aggressive war', which was deliberately excluded from the Statute. He proved that the war in Kosovo had all the three essential elements which every crime s; 1) a criminal act, 2) a criminal intent and 3) a lack of lawful justification or excuse. The war represented a crime against the laws and customs of war since it did not respect the three basic principles; discrimination, necessity and proportionality. To corroborate this statement Professor Mandel quotes the findings of the Amnesty International, which identified three basic types of war crimes committed by NATO. First, attacking civilian targets such as the Belgrade RTS radio and television building. Second, failing to suspend attacks even after it became clear that they would cause loss of civilian life excessive in relation to the concrete military advantage. Examples include killing of civilians on bridges in Grdelica, Luzane and Varvarin. Third, taking insufficient precautions to minimise civilian casualties. Examples include bombings that killed displaced civilians in Djakovica and Korisa.

In the last chapter Professor Mandel explains in detail the creation of the ICC (International Criminal Court). Its statue came into force on 1st July 2002 in Rome. Although USA got significant concession such as the exclusion of 'the crime against peace' or aggressive war they together with seven other countries did not sign the Statue. This gave the Americans free hands to undertake unilateral actions and to apply victor's justice or the principle 'Might is Right' to its enemies.

The Holocaust metaphor was mentioned several times in the book. It was used for propaganda purposes to denigrate the Serbs by comparing their crimes to those committed by the Nazis. Apart from propaganda purposes there are some superficial similarities, but also fundamental differences between the overall stance of Nazis and the Serbs.

In 1991 Radovan Karadzic, the leader of the Bosnian Serbs, said in the Bosnian parliament that if the Moslems insisted on independence of Bosnia and Herzegovina this could lead to their disappearance. This resembles Hitler's speech in the Reichstag on 30th January 1939:" If Jewish financiers in Europe and outside Europe manage once more to plunge world into a war, that war will finish neither with a victory for World Jewry or bolshevism, but with annihilation of the Jewish race in Europe". Efficiency, brutality and excellent co-ordination of the Federal army, police forces and paramilitaries in ethnic cleansing in Kosovo matches similar actions of various layers of the Wermacht, Gestapo and Abwehr. However, there are essential differences. Proponents of the Greater Serbia would welcome every Albanian who would say that they had always loved their Serbian homeland. They would love dearly every Croat and Moslem who would declare themselves Serbs of Catholic and Islamic faith respectfully. This was not the case in Nazi Germany. No matter how patriotic German Jews were, and most of them were patriotic, and if they dreamt of the Greater Germany, (Theodor Herzl, the founding father of the Zionist movement, in his youth saw the solution of the Jewish question in the Greater Germany), they were hated by the Nazis. There were numerous examples of German Jews who volunteered to fight in the WWI and who were decorated for their bravery and patriotism, and who in-spite of that found death in Nazi concentration camps. This is fundamental difference between chauvinism and racism. Chauvinism is based on assimilation (what was sometimes named a cultural genocide), racism in its most extreme form is based on extermination.

Chauvinism is a sign of strength, while racism is a sign of weakness. All great empires flourished on chauvinism, not racism. Proponents of the Greater Serbia have never sought racial and religious purity. They tolerate non-Serbs so long as they do not endanger Serb domination.

The book 'How America Gets Away with The Murder' is an excellent analysis of the three wars that USA undertook in the last eight years. Professor Mandel presented a highly sophisticated legal procedure to prove that all the three wars were illegal, aggressive and that therefore represent a crime against humanity. Although the book teems with legal concepts and terms, they are explained meticulously and conclusions of the legal analysis are clear to those outside of the legal profession. This is why the book represents a very attractive read to legal experts as well as to intelligent non-expert readers interested in the topic.

Marko Attila Hoare: "How Bosnia Armed", Saqibooks, London 2004

The book *How Bosnia Armed* is mainly a story about ARBiH (The Army of Bosnia and Herzegovina), according to the author the most controversial and most enigmatic military phenomenon in recent history. The enigma about ARBiH from a military point of view stems from the fact that at the end of the war it emerged neither victorious nor defeated. It remained controversial because its political and ideological aims have never been clearly defined.

Attila Hoare finds a striking similarity between the Partisan movement and ARBiH. At the beginning of the WWII the Partisan movement was multinational, but predominantly Serb in its composition. At the beginning of the Bosnian war ARBiH was multinational, but predominantly Muslim. The Partisan movement protected Serbs from genocide. ARBiH protected Muslims from genocide. At the beginning of the WWII Partisans collaborated with Chetniks before they became enemies. At the beginning of the Bosnian war ARBiH collaborated with HVO (the Croatian Defence Council) before they started fighting each other, especially in 1993. As WWII progressed more Muslims and Croats joined the Partisans so that at the end of the war the movement became genuinely multinational. On the other hand, ARBiH experienced increased national homogenisation, so that at the end of the war it became not only the army of one nation, but also the army of one political party, SDA (the Party of Democratic Action). The largest part of the book is devoted to the analysis of the external and internal factors which contributed to national homogenisation of the ARBiH.

ARBiH was created at the beginning of the war from disparate units such as TO (Territorial Defence), the Patriotic League, the Green berets, MUP (police forces) and various paramilitary groups. Unlike its Serb and Croat counterparts it lacked weaponry, internal cohesion and above all clear political aims and military strategy and tactics. Before the war the clash erupted between TO and the Patriotic League regarding military strategy. The Patriotic League advocated a more aggressive approach towards JNA (The Yugoslav People's Army). Their leaders, especially Sefer Halilovic, later commanding the Chief Staff of the ARBiH, suggested encircling the barracks of the JNA and disarming the soldiers and officers in order to obtain necessary weaponry. The political leadership of SDA with Alija Izetbegovic adopted a conciliatory approach towards the JNA. They wanted to co-operate with the JNA, hoping that the federal army would protect all the citizens of the Republic. Muslim leaders in East Bosnian towns foiled the plan of the Patriotic League to destroy bridges on the river Drina on 25th February 1992. TO handed in its weapons to the JNA. The weapons were later used to shell Sarajevo.

Izetbegovic's conciliatory approach towards the JNA resembles the approach adopted by the Chilean president Salvadore Allende. Having the experience of the Spanish Civil War, where the majority of the officers sided the nationalists, Allende wanted to develop a friendly relationship with the army. He even gave General Pinochet extraordinary responsibilities to protect the country in a situation of crisis.

In both the Chilean and the Bosnian case a co-operation with the army was not possible since army and political leadership pursued entirely different political goals. In other words it was naivete beyond comprehension. Marko Attila Hoare expresses it succinctly with the following passage on page 61:"....... General Divjak, writing after the war and his own retirement, has described Izetbegovic and the Bosnian political leadership in these days as guilty of "defeatist behaviour" and of "incompetence and superficial knowledge and monitoring of the military and political situation ", for "How else to describe the early assessment of the situation by those in responsible positions in the government? First, that there would be no war in Bosnia and Herzegovina; then that while it was possible that the war would break out, it could never do so in Sarajevo; after which they said that an agreement would be reached with the JNA to transform part of the force into the TO of the Republic of Bosnia and Herzegovina!", For a competent professional former JNA officer like Divjak the last of these aspirations was particularly laughable".

Confusion within the ranks of the ARBiH was increased at the beginning of the war when Muslims, former JNA officers defected from the federal army and offered their services to the Bosnian government. They were mistrusted and suspected as KOS (Counter intelligence service) agents. Marko Attila Hoare reveals interesting details which show that KOS tried to influence the political life in BiH even after the international recognition. The parts of the book describing the activities of KOS agents and double agents, sitting on the fence and waiting for who was going to win the war, resemble most suspenseful thrillers.

There were three currents in the ARBiH. The first one consisted of former JNA officers, who were brought up in the spirit of "Brotherhood and Unity" and who wanted the ARBiH to be built as a genuine multinational military force. The second current espoused a sort of a secular Muslim nationalism, similar to Zionism. The third one wanted to create an exclusively Muslim army, whose moral and spiritual development would rely on the principles of the Islamic faith. Owing to the combination of external and internal factors it was the third current which would eventually prevail.

The first blow to the multinational character of the ARBiH was dealt by VOPP (Vance-Owen peace plan). According to this plan Bosnia and Herzegovina was supposed to be divided into 10 semi-autonomous provinces along ethnic lines. Croats were delighted with the plan since their three provinces were given 30% of the country's territory. Muslims initially accepted the plan, according to which they were supposed to cede some territory to Croats and in return gain some land which was under Serb control. But when Serbs refused the plan Muslims did not want to give up the territory under their control to Croats. A fierce fighting broke out between the ARBiH and HVO in which both sides committed atrocities against civilians.

A further blow to a multinational character of the ARBiH was dealt by the Owen-Stoltenberg plan. This plan envisaged a swap of territories, putting Sarajevo under the UN administration and the eventual right of the Serb and Croat entities to secede and join Serbia and Croatia respectively. Although Izetbegovic refused the plan it seemed at the end of 1993 and in the beginning of 1994 that the international community was willing to endorse a full partition of the country and the creation of greater Serbia, greater Croatia and a rump Bosnian state with a Muslim majority. In this atmosphere the Muslim leadership started purging the Bosnian army, police forces and political institutions from non-Muslims. Jovan Divjak, a deputy commander of the ARBiH was dismissed and retired. Dragan Vikic, the legendary defender of Sarajevo, lost his place as the commander of the special police forces and was replaced by a Muslim. Mirko Pejanovic, a Serb member of the BiH presidency also lost his post.

The Washington agreement in March 1994, sponsored by the USA, ended the hostilities between the ARBiH and the HVO. The agreement was a precursor to the formation of the Muslim-Croat federation. It gave a respite to the ARBiH and strengthened it militarily since it envisaged a full co-operation not only with the HVO but also with the Croatian army. However, at the same time it prevented incorporation of the HVO units into the ARBiH. This reinforced an exclusively Mulsim character of the ARBiH.

But it was an internal development which was decisive in national homogenisation of the ARBiH. During the first two years of the war lawlessness reigned in cities and towns controlled by SDA, especially in Sarajevo. Criminal elements within the ARBiH, who enjoyed popularity and the support of Sefer Halilovic, terrorised citizens, especially Serbs and Croats. Izetbegovic was put under pressure to stamp out the criminal elements and to restore law and order. After a fierce battle in which many policemen were murdered the most notorious criminal Musan Topalovic Caco was killed. Stamping out the criminal elements restored law and order and gave more security to ordinary citizens but at the same time strengthened the role of SDA in the ARBIH. From top to the bottom of the army structure people loyal to SDA were given responsibilities. Negative selection went to the extent that commanding positions of the lower units were sometimes given to petty criminals, whose education consisted of three years of primary school. At the same time the ARBiH took the role of a promoter of SDA policy and developed a personal cult of Izetbegovic. All of this took place at the expense of military competence. Attila Hoare records that on the eve of the fall of Srebrenica General Rasim Delic, the commander of the ARBiH, spent the whole day giving a press conference in Sarajevo and in the evening went with his colleagues to a theatre.

In 1992 a prominent Sarajevan, living in London, asked the following question:" There are 15 generals in Sarajevo. Why does Alija Izetbegovic not use their services? Attila Hoare broached the subject on a couple of places in the book. At the beginning of the war the Partisan veterans of all the nationalities condemned the shelling of Sarajevo and offered their services to the Bosnian government. In June 1992 the Bosnian presidency decided to offer the post of the Commander of the General Staff of the ARBiH to General Dzemil Sarac and the posts of his deputies to Generals Mirko Vranic and Milan Acic. However, all of them declined the offer due to their advanced age. At the same time they gave their blessings to the new army and were included in the Military Council, an advisory body attached to the General Staff of the ARBiH. They attended only two sessions of the Council, which proved to be a dysfunctional body. It would be interesting to know, considering the different political and ideological backgrounds, whether Izetbegovic genuinely wanted to use the expertise of the Partisan veterans or was only paying lip-service.

Throughout the book Attila Hoare expresses his sympathies with the ARBiH. He deplores a failure of SDA to appeal to Serbs and Croats and which, together with external developments, led to a national homogenisation of the ARBiH. However, he states that the ARBiH was not entirely innocent. He mentions concentration camps in Celebici, near Konjic and near Visoko in which thousands of Serb and Croat civilians were detained and tortured. Also he mentions atrocities committed by the members of the ARBiH in Central and East Bosnia. These atrocities were, however, on a much smaller scale than those committed by the Serbian and Croatian military forces. Also, they were the result of independent actions of splinter groups, criminal elements within the army, and mujahedeen voluntaries, and were not orchestrated from the top.

In conclusion Attila Hoare states that "the campaign waged by the ARBiH was successful as a Bosnia and Herzegovina liberation struggle, except insofar as Bosnia-Herzegovina's independence was formally recognised by Serbia and Croatia and the international community; it was unsuccessful, however, as a Muslim-Bosniak national-liberation struggle.". The ARBiH also managed to retain control of the country's economic and demographic heartland including three and a half major cities.

Attila Hoare used a wide range of sources; books, archive sources, journals, magazines and newspaper articles. He has a very good command of Bosnian/Serbo-Croat, which enabled him to use more sources in that language than in English. He analysed a specific angle of the Bosnian war and he did it as an objective and competent scholar. The book is warmly recommended to readers.

James Gow: "The Serbian Project and its Adversaries – A Strategy of War Crimes", Hurst & Co. London 2003

The Serbian Project and its Adversaries – A Strategy of War Crimes is one of the many books dealing with the war in the former Yugoslavia. This time the emphasis is on the military-political and to a lesser degree on the legal analysis of the war. Professor Gow considers two concepts of war, the decision to wage war (*ius ad bellum*) and the way it is waged (*ius in bellum*) as the most essential to the ethical conduct of war. In the second chapter entitled "Political and Historical Background" he tries to establish *casus belli* for the conflict in the former Yugoslavia. He perceives the Yugoslav war as a clash of statehood projects. This assessment of the conflict is more accurate and more founded than the alternative ones such as "ancient ethnic hatred" or "clash of civilisations". Since the emphasis is on the Serbian Project professor Gow first traces back the Serbian national and statehood idea to the middle of the XIX century. This idea, expressed in the slogan "All Serbs in one state" came into fruition with the establishment of Yugoslavia. With the break-up of Yugoslavia the Serbian statehood project had to be revised. It took the form of the quest for the new borders in the West, which would comprise as many Serbs as possible. Professor Gow considers this claim legitimate. At the same time he considers the statehood projects of the Serbian adversaries, Slovenes, Croats and Bosnian Muslims to maintain the current borders legitimate too. In this respect according to professor Gow, different statehood projects were irreconcilable and the war was unavoidable. Possible compromising solutions with the view of avoiding the conflict were not discussed, since this was not the subject of the book. Professor Gow wanted to establish the case for the war and he did it in the most concise and elegant way.

The chapter "Political and Historical Background" contains a few minor inaccuracies and typing errors. On page 32 *"It was renamed the Socialist Federative Republic of Yugoslavia in 1974."* It should be in 1947. On page 33 the Bogomils *("lovers of God"). Bogomils mean "dear to God".* However, this does not have any relevance to the nature of the sect since it was named after the XI century Bulgarian priest, whose name was Bogumil. On page 34 *"... in which the South Slavs would be added to the Austrians and Germans as a pillars of the Empire".* It should be Hungarians instead of Germans. On page 41 *"...after the Balkan wars 1911-1913"* It should be 1912-1913. Otherwise professor Gow shows excellent knowledge of the South Slav history and an objective, impartial scholarly approach.

The greatest part of the book is dedicated to the second aspect of the war, *ius in bellum*, or the way war is waged. Professor Gow quotes the famous definition given by von Clausewitz that strategy in its most simple and authentic version is about the creation and application of force to achieve political ends. It is this aspect of the war in the former Yugoslavia, the ends of the war that caused the most outrage in the international community. For the main aim of the Serbian war strategy and to a lesser extent other participants in the conflict was the removal of potentially hostile populations through ethnic cleansing, intimidation, murder, rape and torture. In order to carry out the strategy of war crimes Serbian politicians and professional soldiers had to create and apply force. In spite of losses of some military stock in Slovenia, Croatia and Bosnia and Herzegovina, Serbs inherited 80% of the military potential of the JNA, one of the strongest armies in Europe. In the meantime, Serbs obtained some weapons from the West and from the countries of the former Eastern block such as Russia Ukraine and East Germany. At the beginning of the war Serbs had an overwhelming military superiority. For example, Republika Srpska, the Serbian entity in Bosnia and Herzegovina, had more tanks than the whole British army. The ratio between weapons held by the Serbs and Muslims at the beginning of the war in Bosnia and Herzegovina was at least 10 to 1. In such a situation Serbs felt comfortable to apply force to achieve their aims. With international recognition of Croatia and Bosnia and Herzegovina a legal problem emerged. Former JNA had to be transformed from the communist and multi-ethnic to professional and essentially Serb army. At the same time JNA was divided into three parts; VJ (The Yugoslav Army), which was the official army of the newly created Federal republic of Yugoslavia, VRS (The Army of the Republika Srpska), which was the Bosnian Serb army and OSRSK, which was the army of the Krajina Serbs in Croatia. The division of the former JNA was accompanied by withdrawal of the officers from Serbia from Croatia and Bosnia and their replacement by Croatian Serb and Bosnian Serb officers respectively. This move was supposed to create the illusion that Belgrade was not involved in the war and that therefore there was no aggression, but only internal conflict in Croatia and Bosnia and Herzegovina. In fact, all the three parts of the transformed JNA were one entity. Officers in VRS and OSRSK were appointed, paid and replaced by Belgrade. They received aid from VJ and were subordinated to it throughout the war. Apart from VJ, VRS and OSRSK Serb forces included MUP (police forces) and various paramilitary groups and militias.

Having achieved the overwhelming military superiority Serbs felt confident that they would achieve their war aims. The only factor which could spoil their project was a potential external intervention by NATO. Serb military experts carefully analysed the Gulf war and tried to draw relevant conclusions. The overall conclusion was that the Gulf war was a unique event and that it was unlikely that it would be repeated in the Balkans. The most important reason for this was the fact that the Balkans was not the sphere of interest of the USA. It is much more important for the Western European countries. If Western European countries decided to strike without USA backing, Serb military experts were confident that the FRY would be able to withstand the attack.

Professor Gow gives a detailed analysis of military operations in Croatia, Bosnia and Herzegovina and Kosovo. In Croatia, there were three sub-theatres of operations. One was in the east, close to the border along the river Danube between Croatia and Serbia. A second was in the far south, along the thin strip of the Dalmatian cost surrounding the town of Dubrovnik and bordering on Montenegro and eastern Herzegovina. The third sub-theatre was the largest, incorporating the Serb-heartland of Krajina and regions to the north of it. The key initial objective, based around the Serb-populated areas, was to break Croatia in two. The more that Serbian action could disrupt north-south communications in Croatia, the weaker Croatia's position would be.

In Bosnia and Herzegovina the principal objective of the Serbian armed forces at the beginning of the campaign was to take control of entry or major communication points. This is why in the first weeks all the major conflicts occurred at places such as Bijeljina or Visegrad, whose control was of vital importance for the Serbian armed forces in order to enable free access for Serbian movements. This strategy left the core of the country surrounded by the Serbian forces under the operational plan "RAM" (meaning frame). The frame was established around periphery of the country from which non-Serbs and disloyal Serbs were expelled.

While in Croatia and Bosnia and Herzegovina the Serbian aim was to annex significant territories to Serbia, in Kosovo the aim was to maintain the old borders. In the long run it would be difficult to achieve this aim when more than 90% of the population of the province were ethnic Albanians. The Serbian strategy in Kosovo was therefore to ethnically cleanse, if not the whole province, then at least the northern parts close to Serbia. In 1998 a limited ethnic cleansing was undertaken, which saw 300,000 ethnic Albanians displaced within the province. The Serbian authorities were careful not to cross a threshold which would attract the attention of the international community. Professor Gow argues that Slobodan Milosevic wanted the NATO intervention to materialise. This would give him a justification for a full-scale ethnic cleansing.

So, what in such a situation was the hope of the Serbian local adversaries? One, implicitly mentioned in the book, was that the Serbs would never fight with a full military potential (for example, there could never be a full mobilisation in Serbia). The second one was, that at certain point in the conflict there would be a NATO intervention.

In Slovenia, the main strategy was to avoid a frontal conflict and to engage the enemy in a short campaign with a big impact. This was accompanied by a strong media campaign, whose aim was to show the world that Slovenes were ready to fight.

Croatian aims were ambiguous throughout. On one side Croatia wanted to preserve its borders, on the other side it looked for the annexation of the parts of Bosnia and Herzegovina with Croat Majority. Croatian forces consisted of HV (a Regular Croatian army), HVO (Croatian Defence Council), Croatian forces in Bosnia and Herzegovina, Ministry of Interior Special Forces and paramilitary groups such as HOS and Black Legion. In the beginning of the war Croatian strategy was to portray themselves as victims of Serbian aggression. A wanton destruction and fall of Vukovar helped to build this picture when authorities in Zagreb persistently refused to send help to the defenders of the town.

Bosnian Muslims co-operated with the JNA in efforts to disarm all paramilitary groups and to place the weapons of the Bosnian Territorial defence under army control. The attempt to avoid war was futile and Bosnian Muslims found themselves defenceless at the beginning of the war. Armed forces, built immediately before and during the war, consisted of ABiH (official BiH army), the Patriotic League, a private army of the ruling party, MUP and paramilitary groups such as Green Berets. Rank and file fought bravely and achieved several military feats. In spite of this a lack of weapons and incompetence of military leaders throughout the war left the ABiH the weakest side in the conflict and most dependent on foreign military intervention.

Dependence on foreign military intervention was even more pronounced in a strategy of Kosovo Albanians. For many years Albanians, under the leadership of Ibrahim Rugova, pursued a policy of passive resistance. In the mid1990s this policy was abandoned and replaced by a more militant approach. The main armed force UCK (Liberation Army of Kosovo) numbered several thousand soldiers. It achieved a few military successes near the Albanian border, but in all major clashes was badly beaten by the Serbian forces. Thus, the only hope for Albanians remained a NATO intervention.

The last chapter of the book is dedicated to the analysis of the international adversaries to the Serbian project. On the strategic level the aim of international participants of the conflict was to preserve the territorial integrity of Croatia and Bosnia and Herzegovina and to prevent a humanitarian disaster. On a tactical level the involvement ranged from providing humanitarian aid and peacekeeping in Croatia and Bosnia and Herzegovina to direct military actions in Bosnia and Herzegovina and Kosovo. In August and September 1995 NATO strikes against Serbian positions in Bosnia and Herzegovina broke Serbian communications and speeded up the end of the conflict. In Kosovo NATO waged a 78 day war with Serbia with a view of reversing the results of the Serbian campaign of ethnic cleansing.

In the part related to Kosovo professor Gow reveals an interesting detail about the *Rambouillet agreement*. Many circles in the West accused USA and NATO for giving the ultimatum to the Serbs. There were two clauses in the agreement which no country in the world would consent to. The first one was about a referendum on Kosovo independence after an interim period of three years. The second one was a military annex, according to which NATO troops would have freedom of movement and access to all facilities on the whole territory of the FRY. After the end of hostilities both clauses were ditched. This is why Serbs understood the signing of the truce as a military defeat and a political victory. Professor Gow did not mention the clause on the referendum. As far as the military annex is concerned he calls it a lazy copy from the Bosnian case. However, he denies that there was an ultimatum. Allegedly, it was only a proposal subject to negotiations. He claims that even Madeleine Albright was personally involved. According to Professor Gow she offered Milosevic a pen, asking him to change in the annex everything what was unacceptable to the Serbian side. Milosevic defiantly folded arms, refusing to discuss the matter. Professor Gow drew a conclusion that Milosevic wanted a NATO attack. He estimated that the assault would last not more than three weeks and that Serbia would withstand the attack and carry on with a full scale ethnic cleansing.

The book is an excellent analysis of the war in the former Yugoslavia. Professor Gow provided a detailed military-political and to a lesser degree legal and historical analysis of the war. His military analysis on strategic and tactical and operational level is particularly impressive. He sticks to well-founded facts and draws unbiased and scholarly objective conclusions.

Professor Gow used a wide range of resources; books, newspaper articles, interviews, even unpublished PhDs. The literature presented is in four languages; English, Serbo-Croat/Bosnian, French and Spanish. It is shame that he did not give a bibliography at the end of the book. This would make life easier to those who would like to conduct further research.

The book is strongly recommended to everyone interested in the Balkans.

Slobodan Markovich, Eric Beckett Weaver and Vukasin Pavlovic (editors):"Challenges to New Democracies in the Balkans", The Associaltion of Fulbright Alumni of Serbia and Montenegro and Cigoja Press in collaboration with the Anglo-Yugoslav Society, Belgrade 2004

The book *Challenges to New Democracies in the Balkans* is a collection of 8 articles divided into three sections. The first section, called **Consolidation** consists of three articles. The second section called **Heritage** also consists of three articles, while the third section called **Globalisation** contains two articles.

In her article *"Democratic Consolidation:Political, Economic and Social Dimension"*, Professor Margaret Blunden distinguishes between democratic transition and democratic consolidation. While electoral democracy is sufficient to achieve democratic transition a fully developed liberal democracy is needed to achieve democratic consolidation. Democratic consolidation, according to the author, is a long process which might take a whole generation rather than a decade. There are serious impediments to democratic consolidation in the Balkans such as historical legacy of authoritarianism, the absence of the rule of law, insecure property and human rights, and the largely illiberal cultural traditions of the both Orthodox Church and Islam as well as a longstanding divide, socially, materially and educationally, between the countryside and the cities. In addition, a social basis of liberal democracy has been weakened by the exodus of 300,000 highly educated graduates from the University of Belgrade. On the positive side Professor Blunden points out some familiarity with the market economy, the asset of a highly educated and talented elite, a strong network of NGO organisations, and a relatively free press.

In the article *"Democratic Consolidation – Revisited"* Joseph V. Julian states that while people in new democracies in the Balkans appreciate the principles of liberal democracy, they are increasingly concerned about the way it works. This is related to a disappointment which the changes brought, such as deteriorating economic situation accompanied by a fall in the standard of living and increased insecurity. He quotes Jean Jacques Rousseau who once said:" Freedom is a food easy to eat but hard to digest". Disappointment with a newly acquired freedom could lead to what Erich Fromm succinctly described in the title of his famous book *Escape from Freedom*. This is already happening in some countries in a mild form through political passivity expressed by a low turn-out during elections. According to the author this trend could be reversed by the strengthening of civil society and greater participation of citizens in policy making.

In the article *"Political Socialisation as a Means of Consolidating Pluralism and Democracy in South-Eastern Europe"* George Voskopoulos states that political socialisation and political awareness will assist the formulation of social groups which compete in a pluralist society. This is of the utmost importance since the existence of various social groups with different interests is the essential precondition of a pluralist society. Voskopoulos claims that these groups were either non-existent or marginalised during the communist era. He ascribes a vital role to education and independent media in raising political awareness of citizens and promoting the political culture of a civil society.

All the above-mentioned articles more or less emphasise a long authoritarian tradition, a lack of the rule of law, independent media and a civil society in the Balkan countries. This is contrasted with the presence of all these elements in "mature Western democracies". Such an approach implicitly leads to a conclusion that the Balkan countries should look for a role model in the West. However, a closer inspection makes the existence of such a role model questionable.

In the big Western countries the media are part of a corporate structure. The aim of the most of them is not to raise political awareness of citizens or to promote civil political culture but to maximise profit so that big shareholders can be satisfied with their dividends and capital gains and managers with high salaries, perks and bonuses. Of course there are newspapers, even the national ones, whose aim is to raise political awareness of citizens. But they are read by a small fraction of readers who have an already developed political culture and who only need additional information and possibly journalists' opinions on particular issue. A research of the freedom and independence of the press in 21 developed countries whose results were mentioned in Naomi Chomsky's book *America's Quest for Global Dominance – Hegemony or Survival* show that the USA is in the 17th and the UK in the 15th place. Norway is in first place, but it can hardly be a role model because of its size and apparent lack of such an ambition.

Quoting ancient Greek philosophers and historians such as Plato, Aristotle and Herodotus, when talking about citizens' political participation is misplaced because of the fundamentally different nature of ancient and modern parliamentary democracy. A Greek *polis* (city-state) was a small community in which free citizens could have a direct influence on political decisions. This is not the case in a modern parliamentary democracy. There are numerous examples which can prove a total exclusion of citizens from vital political decisions. In Spain and the UK only 10% and 11% of the population respectively supported the war in Iraq. Genuinely democratic leaders would put a decision about the war to a referendum. In the UK capital punishment was abolished although 75% of the population were against that decision. Thus the decision to abolish capital punishment was not democratically arrived at. It was imposed by liberal and leftist elite. When assessing "mature Western democracies" it would be more appropriate to say that from the French Revolution onwards they have experienced the strengthening of the process of undemocratic liberalism. The coinage "liberal democracy" very often taken for granted can very often be *contradiction in adiecto*.

In his long and excellent article entitled *"The Political and Economic Heritage of modern Serbia":Two centuries of convergence and divergence between Serbia and Western Europe"*, Slobodan G. Markovich analysis a classical example of dichotomy between democracy and liberalism in Serbia in the last two decades of the 19th century. Serbian peasantry was passionately democratic, but hostile to the alien liberal principles imported from the West. A burgeoning capitalist class and intellectuals educated in the West tried to impose liberal principles on Serbian society with the use of undemocratic methods.

In the article *"National Minorities and New Democracies:The "Ethnic Revival" and Majoritarian Democracy"* Professor Vojislav Stanovcic argues that liberal democracy is less successful in safeguarding ethnic rights than in providing individual human rights. He claims that multiculturalism and multi-ethnicity can become an obstacle to democracy. To corroborate this statement he quotes John Stuart Mill who in his work *On Representative Government* said that in a country which consists of several nationalities, free institutions of a representative government were "next to impossible". Nevertheless, Professor Stanovcic gives better chances to democracy than authoritarian regimes to tackle the ethnic problem. The latter, by restricting individual rights and strengthening etatist trends actually generates ethnic conflicts.

In the article *"Madness in the Media:Political Extremism and Beliefs in Historical Primacy as a Feature of Transition"* Eric Beckett Weaver researches the influence of religious myths, beliefs and customs on building national megalomania and the development of pseudo-scientific theories of national superiority. He claims that in the transition countries this phenomenon is most noticeable in Hungary. Although this trend is present in the West it is more pronounced in Eastern Europe. The author explains this by a weak publishing market in Eastern Europe and the dependence of the publishers' revenue on private financiers and political parties rather than from the readers.

In the article *"Globalisation, Democracy and Civil Society":The Democratic and Authoritarian Face of Globalisation"* Professor Vukasin Pavlovic analysis different theories of democratisation and globalisation and tries to find the one which would be the most applicable to Serbia. He argues that liberalisation, democratisation and consolidation should be perceived as parts of the same process if liberal democracy is to be established. He suggests that a combination of top-down political strategies and bottom-up social strategies need to be pursued if democratic consolidation is to be successful in Serbia.

In the article *"Civil Society, Multi-ethnic Conflicts and Globalisation"* Professor Radmila Nakarada analyses the effects of globalisation on multi-ethnic conflicts in different societies. She argues globalisation in its neo-liberal version generates ethnic conflicts by attacking solidarity and human considerations. Feeling increasingly insecure many people seek a protection shield within their ethnic communities. The solution of the problem, according to Professor Nakarada, lies in the establishment of the global civil society and the global rule of law.

The articles in the book are written by renowned scholars in the fields of Political Sciences, Sociology and History. The book will attract the attention of those who are interested in the Balkans as well as those who have inclinations to explore various theoretical aspects of democracy, liberalism and globalisation.

Elizabeth Pond 'Endgame in the Balkans – Regime Change, European Style', Brookings Institution Press, 2006

The book 'Endgame in the Balkans – Regime Change, European Style' is a rich and profound analysis of the events which followed the fall of communism in the Balkan countries. In the preface of the book Elizabeth Pond states that in order to understand the modern Balkans it is essential to start with two foundation stones: the wars of the Yugoslav succession and the lure of the EU membership that is common to all the former communist countries. The contrast between a bleak and atavistic past, fraught by corruption, authoritarianism, violence and chauvinism and the prospect of modernity, prosperity, democracy and the rule of law pervades the whole book. The main question the book tries to answer is "....... *is the magnetic attraction of EU membership strong enough to pull the Balkans through the pain of reform to the democratic and market "normality" they long for?"*.

The book consists of 11 chapters. The first chapter is entitled:' The Wars of the Yugoslav Succession'. The following eight chapters deal with a recent history of each and every Balkan country: Bulgaria, Romania, Kosovo, Croatia, Bosnia, Macedonia, Albania and Montenegro. The tenth chapter' Europeanizing the Balkans' summarizes the analysis conducted in the previous chapters. The last chapter 'Reaching Critical Mass' provides concluding remarks.

The chapters analyzing 8 Balkan countries start with a brief and concise history. This is used as an explanatory guide to the events which occurred in a recent history. The modern events are described meticulously and accurately in detail. Elizabeth Pond conducted hundreds of interviews in order to get information from a horse's mouth. The use of primary data helped to understand better a difficulty and complexity of the reforms the Balkan countries need to undertake in order to catch up with the rest of Europe.

Elizabeth Pond is aware of obstacles which lie on the road to a full membership in the EU. She revokes the collapse of democracies in the Central Europe in the interwar period and in Latin America in the 1980's to warn against premature euphoria. Still, her view is optimistic. She praises the EU for extraordinary achievements in political sphere. They include reconciliation between France and Germany, the arch enemies and successful consolidation of democratic regimes in Greece, Spain and Portugal, the countries which experienced prolonged dictatorships after the WW2. In the case of the Balkan countries she corroborates her optimism with positive developments in Bosnia stating that many refugees have returned to their homes and that, for example, an acting chief of police in *Republika Srpska* is a Bosniak.

The book is an extremely well researched piece of work. Elizabeth Pond shows an enviable erudition in many areas of social sciences. The sources which she used are equally impressive. There is a long list of 34 pages of references, which include transcripts, websites, reports, files, listings, books and journal articles as well as hundreds of interviews conducted in all the eight Balkan countries. The majority of sources are in English and German, although several of them are in Bosnian/Serbo-Croat.

The book represents a very interesting read in every aspect. It is warmly recommended to readers.

Sumatra Bose:'Bosnia after Dayton – Nationalist Partition and International Intervention', Hurst & Company London 2001, pp 295

The book 'Bosnia after Dayton – Nationalist Partition and International Intervention' is written as a thesis. In introductory pages Professor Bose sets up the main hypothesis of his research by asking the following questions:*Is the preservation of a multinational state desirable in a situation where the vast majority of citizens belonging to two of the three constituent communities of the state only reluctantly acknowledge its legitimacy? Even if desirable is it possible in a context where those two groups taken together constitute around half the state's population, control some 70% of the state's territory, almost all its 'international' borders, and have contiguous 'mother states' to support their claims and act as an alternative focus of loyalty? Or is a formal partition nor just the more realistic but the more just alternative in these circumstances, where communitarian claims to 'self-determination' are not just in conflict but mutually incompatible?'*

Professor Bose gives the affirmative answer to the first two questions. He is in a favour of the preservation of the state of Bosnia and Herzegovina, albeit in a highly decentralized form. He embarks on a lengthy analysis to put the case for the *de iure* a unified Bosnian state.

Professor Bose emphases the complexity of the Bosnian society, which stems from the fact that the country, after losing its independence in the 15th century, was for four centuries at the crossroads of empires and one century a contested land of competing nationalisms.

In order to prove the complexity of any debate about Bosnia and Herzegovina Professor Bose analyses three binary dichotomies:*tolerance-hatred, aggression-civil war* and *integration-partition*. By weighing opposing arguments he draws a conclusion that *tolerance-hatred dichotomy* is a false one. Before the war there were several Bosnia-Herzegovinas. Bosnia remains a complex and plural society, not only in national but also in many other senses. Tolerance, hate, love, coexistence and fear are all equally present.

The second dichotomy *aggression-civil war* reflects a fundamental debate over the legitimacy of the sovereignty and the borders of the state recognized in April 1992 by the International Community. That question is complex and cannot be unequivocally resolved. However, Professor Bose claims that the conflict in Bosnia and Herzegovina had strong elements of the civil war. In-spite of the external foreign involvement, which accompanies more or less every civil war, the vast majority of the war operations were carried out by the Bosnians. This is a strong proof that the conflict was essentially a civil war.

The third dichotomy *integration-partition* is directly derived from the first two. Scholars and political scientists who stress out a tolerance between the three Bosnian communities and who think of the Bosnian war as a war of aggression are integrationists. They advocate the abandonment of the Dayton Peace Accord and centralization of the state of Bosnia and Herzegovina. Those who emphasize hatred and fear as the major characteristics of life in Bosnia and Herzegovina and who think of the war as a civil war are in favour of a full, *de iure* partition of the country. Professor Bose states that the both sides miss the point. Integrationists overlook the fact that the break-up of Yugoslavia left a large number of Serbs outside the 'mother state'. Their claim for redrawing borders or at least decentralizing their new states is therefore legitimate. Partitionists overlook infeasibility and a huge human cost of partition. Many pages are allocated to the analysis of the partition of the Indian subcontinent in 1947 into two states, India and Pakistan, which produced tragic consequences. Half a million people were killed and 20 million were forcibly displaced. Professor Bose tackles partitionists' 'security dilemma'. Unlike them, he claims that the disappearance of the central power, which guaranteed security to all citizens, led to partition and opened a vicious circle of violence, not other way around. Partition of India, Ireland and Yugoslavia corroborate this thesis.

Professor Bose states that had it not been for the intervention of the International Community it would not have been the state of Bosnia and Herzegovina in its current borders. He fully supports the liberal international intervention in Bosnia and Herzegovina. In different places in the book he gives reasons for this support:

1. Forty five years of modernization and secularization under the communist rule made societies in the Balkans essentially not different from Western societies.
2. There is nothing artificial about Bosnia as an integrated entity. Its geography, shape and economic structure are the cases for integration, not partition. The regions in Bosnia complement each other and without national divisions gravitational pull is towards integration.
3. With a lapse of time it is expected that co-operation between the neighbouring countries will strengthen. Banja Luka naturally gravitates towards Zagreb, Tuzla towards Belgrade and Mostar towards Split. Closer links between the Yugoslav successor states will beef up the edifice of the Bosnian state.
4. Identities are variable over a period of time and multiple. For example, Bosnian Serbs are Bosnians and Serbs at the same time. Their identity is different from identities of the other Bosnians as well as from identity of Serbs in Serbia.

Professor Bose praises the Dayton Peace Accord and its model of a multi-layered sovereignty. Although imperfect, in his opinion the Accord is the only solution for a deeply divided multiethnic society. A whole chapter of the book is allocated to explanation and analysis of structure of the Dayton state. Advantages and disadvantages of a consociational system, enshrined in the Accord are analysed in detail. A major drawback of the system is that it is undemocratic and that excludes individuals who do not identify themselves with main ethnic groups.

One way to strengthen a multiethnic state is through engineering of the electoral system. The whole chapter of the book is dedicated to the analysis of the electoral systems alternative to the majoritarian voting system:open lists, alternative voting, multi-members groups, preferential voting etc. Professor Bose stresses out limitations of these voting systems in multiethnic states.

The book was written in 2001. As far as events, data and figures are concerned it is somewhat outdated. However, the book is highly academic. Discussions about partition, consociational system, various electoral systems and national and multi-national federation have permanent value.

The book is in every respect a very interesting read. It will attract attention of those who are interested in the Balkans as well as the readers who have a passion for various aspects of legal and political theory.

Neven Andjelic: "Bosnia-Herzegovina, the End of Legacy", Frank Cass Publishers, London 2003

The book *Bosnia –Herzegovina, the End of a Legacy,* by the author Neven Andjelic, published in 2003, covers a field of research already explored by many writers. However, this time we come across a direct witness of the events which preceded a bloody war in Bosnia and Herzegovina. As a journalist of a weekly magazine *Nasi Dani (Our Days)* and someone who had a close relationship with political activist of the Liberal Party (former Socialist Youth Organisation) Andjelic provides information from the horse's mouth. This gives him a comparative advantage to other writers whose research has been mainly based on secondary data.

On one occasion Andjelic mentioned that parts of his doctoral thesis are included in the book. The book is actually written as a thesis. In a very long introduction, which has more than 20 pages, Andjelic sets several hypotheses. The rest of the book is elaboration of the main ideas with extensive use of primary and secondary data. The main ideas which Andjelic formulated as hypotheses could be summarised as follows:

It has been popular amongst journalists and politicians in the West, and even more widespread amongst ordinary people to explain the war in former Yugoslavia and Bosnia and Herzegovina in terms of "tribalism" and "ancient ethnic hatred". Scholars, on the other hand are divided into two groups. The first group consists of those who accept the "ancient hatred theory". The second one consists of those who explain the most recent events in Bosnia and Herzegovina in terms of foreign aggression. This group while ignoring the contribution of internal developments to the war draws its arguments from the evidence of mutual co-existence and tolerance of the three ethnic groups throughout history. Andjelic challenges both approaches as simplistic and one-sided.

The main proponent of "The ancient ethnic hatred theory" is the American professor Samuel Huntington. In his famous and much disputed book *The Clash of Civilisations and the Remaking of the World Order* Huntington states that Europe is divided into a Western part, i.e. Protestant and Catholic, and Eastern part, i.e. Orthodox and Moslem. He explains the Bosnian war on religious grounds, as a "fault line war". Andjelic counters Huntington's view with three very strong arguments.

Bosnia and Herzegovina is the clearest example that such a division has never existed. When she was part of the Ottoman Empire Bosnia and Herzegovina belonged culturally to the eastern part of the European continent. When Austria-Hungary occupied and annexed the country it imposed a Western culture, moving the invisible line of the division to the east.

Secondly, the population of Bosnia and Herzegovina has never been divided along cultural lines. Members of the three communities have lived together for centuries in the same cities, villages and even families. Apart from that, regardless of religion, according to Andjelic, members of all the three communities share the same culture.

And thirdly, the strongest argument against Huntington's theory Andjelic finds in decades of communist reign. Communism developed its own system of values, culture and sense of identity. Countries which previously belonged to "Western civilisation" lost many of their old attributes and developed new ones. These new attributes, stronger and more significant than the old ones, are common both to post-communist societies of western Christianity and to those of eastern Christianity, but are completely alien to countries which had not experienced communist rule. Hence, Andjelic concludes, the countries that belonged to western Christianity can hardly have the same type of culture as in the past.

The second group of writers, who explain war in Bosnia and Herzegovina in terms of foreign aggression, is best represented by the

English historian Noel Malcolm. In his book *Bosnia-A Short History*, Malcolm claims that the population in Bosnia and Herzegovina has always lived in harmony, and that all conflicts were the result of external developments and foreign influences. Andjelic challenges this view by a long analysis of internal developments in Bosnia and Herzegovina. He agrees with Malcolm that most of the history of Bosnia and Herzegovina was characterised by tolerance and mutual solidarity. Minor tensions and frictions arose from the fact that Bosnia lost its independence in 1463 and that the three communities had different attitudes towards foreign rulers. However, most of the rebellions had social background such as the peasants' uprising against landowners and high taxes. The first divisions occurred in the 19th century in the period of national romanticism, when religion played the key role in formation of nationhood and prevented a creation of a unified Bosnian nation. The Orthodox population acquired "Serbian national conscience" and the Catholic population acquired "Croatian national conscience". The second division occurred during the Second World War when occupation of the country and the civil war was accompanied by a bloody fratricidal war.

The greatest part of the book Andjelic dedicates to a communist attempt to heal the wounds of the Second World War and to re-establish harmony and tolerance between different ethnic communities. He states that the ethnic policy of "brotherhood and unity" was at the top of the communist agenda. This policy was pursued in all the republics but nowhere more than in Bosnia and Herzegovina. Unlike the other republics, which were defined as nation states, Bosnia and Herzegovina was defined as a state of three constituent nations. Therefore, the ethnic issues were the most sensitive in the central Yugoslav republic.

The policy of "brotherhood and unity" was successfully implemented in Bosnia and Herzegovina for decades. The ethnic harmony was restored with an iron fist and careful, calculated and the well balanced trials of those who threatened inter-ethnic relationships. The implementation of the policy was facilitated by a vigorous economic growth and a huge rise in the standard of living. After Tito's death the policy was continued, although in deteriorating economic conditions. Andjelic stresses the incompetence of the Bosnian politicians in resolving major economic and social problems.

A decisive moment for the ethnic policy of "brotherhood and unity" came in 1987 with the "Agrokomerc scandal". The Agrokomerc scandal caused a great damage to the Bosnian economy and signalled the end of hard-line Bosnian rulers. This opened a door to unprecedented liberalisation of the media and society as a whole. Almost overnight huge, for decades suppressed social energy was released and Bosnia and Herzegovina was transformed from the paragon of dictatorship to a most liberal republic. The new leaders were too weak to control the country. They made the attempt to prevent the formation of national parties, but the pressure was too strong and they had eventually to give in.

Andjelic excellently identified three internal developments which paved a way to the victory of nationalist parties in 1990 elections: predominance of rural communities, with a strong sense of ethnic belonging and national feelings over cosmopolitan city dwellers; a large number of political converts amongst influential intellectuals and the agreement between three major nationalist parties, which gave the impression to many ordinary people that "partnership in power" would bring the country much wanted peace, harmony and prosperity.

When talking about the referendum on independence, which was a prelude to the war, Andjelic correctly stated what most of other writers omitted, that Alija Izetbegović, being a national leader, did not have a legitimacy to schedule a referendum of citizens. Andjelic mentioned Zdravko Grebo's proposal to define Bosnia and Herzegovina as a state of all its citizens. Such a constitutional arrangement can have appeal only to people who do not seek their identity in nationhood (ethnicity) and who identify themselves with a wider supranational entity (European Yugoslav, Bosnian). A state of all citizens means one person one vote and in multi-ethnic states favours the most numerous ethnic group. Even Croats, who overwhelmingly voted for the independence of Bosnia and Herzegovina would not accept such a definition of the Bosnian state. Nation states could be defined as states of all citizens. Such a definition is welcomed by national minorities. They feel more comfortable than if a state in which they live is defined only as a state of one nation.

On several occasions Andjelic repeated that politicians who ruled Bosnia and Herzegovina after Tito's death were incompetent. It is true that the Bosnian politicians in 1980s lacked knowledge and ideas as how to tackle major economic and social problems. However, there were two external developments, which aggravated the economic and social situation in Bosnia and Herzegovina and the whole of Yugoslavia, which Andjelic failed to mention. One of these external developments is economic, the other one is political.

In almost three decades after the Second World War the world economy experienced an unprecedented prosperity. Gross Domestic Product rose by 5.6% and world trade at a staggering 7.3% per annum. Capital and financial aid flew from the core countries to the periphery of the world economy. At the same time developed countries experienced a shortage of labour force and were ready to absorb surpluses of workers from developing countries. In such a situation it was much easier for politicians in developing countries to tackle major economic and social problems. In 1980s the world economy went through a sharp recession. Western creditors demanded repayment of credits with high interests. This put a strain on productive capacities and the standard of living in developing countries.

In the conference in Yalta in 1943 Yugoslavia was divided in the proportion 50:50 between the great powers. Tito skilfully exploited this together with the fact that in 1948 the Soviet Union did not have the atomic bomb. Tito's split with Stalin was generously rewarded by the West. According to some estimates Yugoslavia received in money and kind between 100 and 120 billion dollars. This artificially increased the standard of living in Yugoslavia to the extent that Yugoslav citizens lived much better than their counterparts in more developed Western European countries. With the advent of Michael Gorbachev and political changes in Eastern Europe Yugoslavia lost its privileged status as a buffer zone against the Soviet Bloc.

Of course, there were other resources which Bosnian politicians could have exploited such as remittances of the workers in Western Europe and savings of Yugoslav citizens. Ante Markovic skilfully exploited these resources for a while before his policies were destroyed by nationalist leaders.

The book contains a few minor inconsistencies. On page 15 it is stated"…. a major concession given to the JMO by the Radicals in power was the preservation of Bosnian historical boundaries, which remained unchanged despite a long forgotten medieval independence". The borders of the medieval Bosnian kingdom differed from the borders of the modern Bosnia and Herzegovina. Kulin's Bosnia consisted of Southern, Eastern, North-eastern and Central Bosnia. During Tvrtko's reign, when Bosnia became the most powerful South Slav and the Balkan state, the territory expanded to include the whole of Herzegovina, Central and South Dalmatia and islands and parts of Montenegro and Serbia. However, even at that time a good part of Bosnian and Cazin Krajina were not parts of the kingdom. The borders of the modern Bosnia and Herzegovina were agreed between the Ottoman Empire and Austria in the peace treaty of Pozarevac in 1718 and confirmed by the Congress of Berlin in 1878.

On page 53:"Its main characteristic was the reduction of interest rate with the aim of combating inflation". The aim of reduction in interest rates is to increase spending and investment in order to boost growth and decrease unemployment. If government wants to combat inflation it usually increases interest rates to achieve the opposite; a reduction in consumer spending and investment. But it could be that this is just a typing error.

The book was published in 2003, almost 8 years after the end of war in Bosnia and Herzegovina. It has, therefore a disadvantage that much had already been written on the topic. However, this is more than offset by the advantage stemming from the fact that Andjelic was a witness of more recent events in the history of Bosnia and Herzegovina. This enabled him to supply readers with a more comprehensive and deeper analysis than most other writers and to arrive at more accurate conclusions. Because of that the book is invaluable contribution to the topic and is highly recommended to readers.

Paul Lowe: "Bosnians", Saqi Books in association with the Bosnian Institute, London 2005

The book *Bosnians* is a collection of more than 160 photographs and essays written by various writers, politicians, journalists and professional soldiers about Bosnia and the Bosnian war. The photographs were provided by Paul Lowe and the essays were collected by Allan Little.

Allan Little used as an introduction an extract from the book *Travels in European Turkey, 1850,* by E. Spencer, in which the author expresses his fascination by a beautiful landscape, delightful environs, blooming gardens, rivers and rivulets combined with a plain unsurpassed for fertility in whose midst lays the wealthy town of Sarajevo with its gilded tower, the swelling dome, painted minaret and bazaars roofed with tiles of every shade and colour all glittering in the sun. This beautiful picture is contrasted with what comes later in the book, the horrors of the war.

The book is divided into six parts. The first part, entitled *The Siege*, shows the photographs of Sarajevans trying to escape shells and sniper bullets and those who were wounded and treated in hospitals. They are accompanied by an extract from the book *The Question of Bruno*, by the Bosnian writer Alexander Hemon.

The second part, *The Dead*, shows the photographs of people gathered at graveyards and the grave signs of the killed civilians, many of them children. They are accompanied by gruesome descriptions of decapitated bodies and bloody human flesh detached from the corpses.

The third part, *The Living*, depicts the life of the civilians of Sarajevo under the siege and the struggle for survival under unbearable living conditions:a lack of water, electricity and heating when the temperature dropped to-10 degrees Celsisus, and exorbitant prices of food. In spite of all these deprivations a sort of cultural life was flourishing in Sarajevo during the war with a hoist of art exhibitions, concerts, theatre, and dance performances.

The fourth part, *The Missing*, is devoted to the massacre in Srebrenica and torture and killing of civilians in concentration camps in Manjaca and Omarska.

The fifth part, *The Return*, shows the photographs of destroyed houses and buildings to which refugees decided to return after the war, in spite of all obstacles and dangers.

The last part, *The Survivors*, is dedicated to the period after the war. A slow return to normality is pictured through the photographs of a wedding party, sledging down an icy slope, singing and drinking in a restaurant, skiing on Mt. Bjelasnica and the preparations of the Bosnian Disabled Volleyball Team for the match against Iran, their main international rival.

Bosnians is a photograph exhibition turned into a book. It is not pleasant and enjoyable stuff. The majority of the photographs contain destroyed buildings, graveyards, amputated limbs, artificial arms, bones and skulls. The extracts from Mesa Selimovic's *Death and Dervis* in which he talks about the cursed lands at the crossroads of foreign conquerors and civilisations, and from Ivo Andric's *The Bridge on Drina* in which he talks about the dark side of human nature which is allowed to crop up when all inhibitions are removed, help to explain what happened in Bosnia during the war. The extracts which speak about the love of Bosnians for their country represent an enjoyable reading. So do the extracts which speak about the love foreigners such as the English Miss Irby and Belgian general Francis Briquemont have for Bosnia and its people. And also the words of Allan Little, which in spite of everything that happened in Bosnia raise a hope:"... *But Bosnians will live together again. They will trust each other again. And they will do so because they always have. Ethnic separation makes no sense – not economic, not geographic, not cultural – and the lesson of that whole shameful episode in the history of our continent is that so unnatural is ethnic separation in that part of the world that it could only be achieved through the barrel of a gun. So Bosnia will knit itself together again because there is no alternative. But not yet. Not for a long time. For the end of a war is more traumatic than its start."*

Svetlana Broz:"Dobri ljudi u vremenu zla – Good People in Evil Time", Media Centar "Prelom", Banja Luka, 2003

The book *Good People in Evil Time* begins with memories going back to 1979 when Yugoslavia was a peaceful and prosperous country. Dr Svetlana Broz, at the time a student in the final year of the Faculty of Medicine, prepared for an exam in war surgery. She thought that the subject was only of academic relevance. As far as Yugoslavia was concerned this subject was even out-dated. Twelve years afterwards she was shocked when Yugoslavia broke up in violence and bloodshed. She was particularly disappointed with what she experienced in "cosmopolitan" Belgrade. Friendships were crumbling in futile disputes over whose nationalistic evil was worse.

Dr Svetlana Broz refused to believe that the material and spiritual destruction of her country annihilated everything good and noble in human beings. She decided to go to Bosnia to help the victims of the war. Working as a cardiologist, she listened to stories of people who found themselves on the wrong side of the barricade and had to experience enormous sufferings. They had burning desires to tell the truth about people who helped them to survive, exposing their lives to mortal danger. Those unknown heroes, who refused national homogenisation dictated by the nationalistic leaders; those who retained humanity at the risk of being labelled as "national traitors" involved in helping the "enemy".

The book contains over 90 stories perceiving human nature through the oldest metaphysical principle of philosophy of history: the struggle between good and evil. Unlike many other books on the war in the former Yugoslavia portraying hatred and evil, this book is focused on the good and noble in human nature. To find drops of good and noble in the ocean of hatred and evil means to believe in Vico's concept that history has a two-stage movement. According to this concept the good and the evil co-exist. They overtake each other through different phases. During periods of advanced human development, the good slowly and gradually take over.

Two stories in this book particularly appeal to me. In the story entitled "Big Shepherds with a Lot of Sheep" (p.53-67), Dr Ante Jelic from Vares talks about his painful experiences during the war. He was a renowned physician of Croatian origin. He was loved and respected by his friends and patients regardless of their ethnicity. When 250 Muslim civilians were imprisoned in 1993 he tried to help them, but was brutally treated by the Croatian militiamen. When the predominantly Muslim BiH Army overrun Vares, he left his native town together with his family. In Kiseljak, controlled by the Croats, Dr Ante Jelic, was harassed and kept in prison for two days. When he decided to return back to Vares, his Muslim neighbours and friends welcomed him. They offered him to work in a medical centre. This infuriated a newly appointed Muslim mayor of the town. Dr Ante Jelic decided to accept the offer, believing that the good of his friends was stronger than the evil of a powerful, politically influential mayor.

In the other story entitled "Don't Give Me Away Mummy", (p. 150-162), Senada Mehmedovic describes her sufferings when the war engulfed Visegrad. She was imprisoned, beaten and disparaged by the local Serb thugs. One of her Serb neighbours helped her to escape and drove her off to a territory controlled by the Muslims. She later learned that her Serb neighbour and his three brothers were killed by the same people who tortured her, for helping the "enemy". When she thought that her nightmare was over she was again imprisoned and beaten, this time by Muslim soldiers.

The message carried by such stories is simple and clear. There are no good and evil nations. The good and the evil are never collective, but are always individual. They are sometimes intertwined in the same person. In the story entitled "This is the Balkans" (p.83-88), Ilija Covic, a Croat from Konjic tells how his drunken Muslim neighbour tried to kill him. A few days later the same man took his pregnant wife to hospital.

The evil is often caused by ignorance and fear. The nationalistic leaders created the impression that all means are justified in the "struggle for survival" against the "collective evil" of the other nations. Tightly controlled media played a vital role in this highly unethical political game. The truth is that the "collective evil" of other nations is nothing else but an individual evil of nationalistic leaders and war profiteers who benefitted at the expense of the tragedy of their own people. This view is succinctly expressed by a Serb policeman who said to his Muslim neighbour (p 36):"This is neither our war not yours".

The ideas on the good and the evil espoused in this book are not new. They sound stereotypical and pathetic, but never worn out. They raise the hope that Vico's concept of good and evil is realistic and that the good will eventually take over. They make a significant contribution to reconciliation amongst the three warring communities. That is the greatest value of the book and Dr Svetlana Broz deserves full credit for her brave and noble efforts.

Vahida Demirovic:"Visage from the Wasteland", Genie Quest Publishing, UK, 1998

The book "Visages from the Wasteland" is a volume of stories dealing with persons whose lives were wrecked by the violent conflict in Bosnia and Herzegovina from 1992 to 1995. It is full of testimonies of brutalities and atrocities committed during this internecine fratricidal warfare. Reports of mass killings, detention of civilians, rapings, ethnic cleansing and destruction of property and sacral objects, which had filled the front pages of the most famous newspapers for years, are present in different forms in such stories from Bosnia. However, the political and legal aspects of the conflict are beyond the scope of this book. Dr Demirovic is not interested in supra-personal facets of International Law and Politics. Neither is she an objective and detached psychoanalyst. She is emotionally and psychologically deeply involved in the personal traumas and sufferings of her patients.

The angle from which the war was perceived is one of a Bosnian physician and humanist, who set herself almost an impossible task: to heal deep psychological wounds inflicted upon the characters of these stories. Dr Demirovic appears in a double role as a humanist and mother healer and as a conveyor of universal ethical messages. In the first role she emphasises the soft and vulnerable souls of her characters. She introduces the reader to a story and starts a dialogue with a character. But the dialogue very often ends up in a monologue, as a method of healing wounds deeply imprinted in the victim's psyche. Through monologues we learn about Umsha's euphoric reminiscences of the village life before the war, Sead's hallucinations, Mara's lethargy and Zuhdija's paranoia. Whatever the form of expression of their pain and suffering, one must be overwhelmed by the stoicism and the quiet dignity with which the characters bear their misfortune. There is neither the curse of individual fate, nor the feeling of victimhood, so often present among the Balkan nations. But what impresses most is the total absence of hatred to perpetrators. Dr Vahida Demirovic, in her second role, through a monologue of a character in the story" Unusual Policeman (p. 55-65), conveys an important message:*My father would never hate anybody. He only hated the bad things they did. He always stresses that hatred only poisons your soul but does not do a thing to your enemy. If hatred helped you make your enemy better or turned him into your friend, there would be a reason for hating him. But hatred only poisons you, leaving you with as big enemy as before, your hatred just eats away at you from inside and makes your smaller... "Animals hate each other; that's why they don't live very long. I mean, the majority of predatory animals have short lives, because their hatred exhausts their life energy. Because hatred is an ulcer on your soul, an ulcer which eats away until it consumes you. And I don't want my soul to be eaten away by an ulcer."*

Allowing a long monologue to unfold, Dr Demirovic identifies herself with the victim. It seems that the victim conveys the message on her behalf. But when a victim's opinion is different from hers she is explicit in expressing her own message. Unlike Edin, a character in the story:"*A Real Life Horror Film*" *(p. 35-44),* who said:" *Our people can survive only if they continue to forget*", Dr Demirovic writes:"*The torture, rape slaughtering and ethnic cleansing which the Bosnian people were exposed to must never be forgotten*".

The characters do not ask for revenge. Punishment is left to perpetrators and their consciences. One of the characters expresses it as:"*All I have left is the hope that at least one of those butchers, wherever he may be, will come to his senses and incriminate himself. And by doing so, he will prove to those of us left alive that he once belonged to the human race, to the species of man*". (p. 44). The message is humanistic and universally ethical. Its aim is to remind us of what irrational forces nationalistic hatred can stir up and what evil human beings can do to each other. So that in the future humankind would do everything to prevent such atrocities and horrors from ever happening again.

"Visages from the Wasteland" is recommended to everybody who is concerned with the crisis of humanity and the dark side of human nature.

www.ingramcontent.com/pod-product-compliance
Lightning Source LLC
Chambersburg PA
CBHW030748180526
45163CB00003B/943